TWO WORLDS HANDBOOK

TWO WORLDS COMMUNITY
FOUNDATION

Vernon D. Swaback, FAIA FAICP

© 2010 Two Worlds Community Foundation
7750 East McDonald Drive
Scottsdale, Arizona 85250
www.TwoWorldsFoundation.org
info@twoworldsfoundation.org

Publisher: Two Worlds Media
Cover and Book Design: Nicholas Markwardt
ISBN 978-1-4507-1927-8

Printed in the United States of America

Inspired by the science and beauty of nature, this work is dedicated to all who support the educational design and stewardship of creation by how we live and build in the here and now.

Also by Vernon D. Swaback:

Designing the Future

The Custom Home
Dreams • Desire • Design

The Creative Community
Designing for Life

Designing With Nature

Creating Value
Smart Development and Green Design

Believing in Beauty

Living in Two Worlds
The Creative Path to Community

CONTENTS

VISION AND MISSION

The Foundation's mission is to create an urgency for life-sustaining design by way of educating, illustrating and accelerating the transition from humanity's current self-defeating trajectory to that of co-creating with nature, all accomplished within the time remaining for that to be possible.

INTRODUCTION

After the final no comes a yes. And on that yes, the future of the world depends.

—Wallace Stevens

This handbook and the fundamental idea it represents is all about understanding the consequences and relationships between what we are doing today and what these activities are shaping for the realities of tomorrow. It is about exploring and understanding the difference between the kinds of positive progress upon which our civilization depends from that which threatens our future.

To think in two worlds is to differentiate between needs that appear obvious from those that may seem less so but are essential. As an example, the provocations that lead to battle can seem too obvious to ignore, while the essential need to live in community may seem too nebulous to engage our all-out commitment. Everything about the pursuit of a sustainable human future requires that we move from exploiting the marketable pieces and products of civilization to nurturing the designed integration and behaviors of community. It is nothing less than applying insights from the world of design to the design of the world. To fail in this pursuit, is to remain on our present trajectory toward institutional and ecological decline. To the extent that we are willing and able to launch an all-out commitment to succeed, the creation of a sustainable society has the potential to become the most joyful, wealth-creating period in human history.

It would be a rare institution or publication that hasn't been admonishing us to design, build and live in ways that are Smart, Green, and Sustainable. Most provide some form of near standard checklist of recommended systems and products. There is less emphasis, and far less understanding, concerning two more fundamental challenges. The first is to recognize the power of design to influence sustainable human behavior. A sustainable future depends far more on behavioral advancements than anything that can be addressed by products or technologies, no matter how innovative they may be.

The second challenge requires a conscious shift in values. Simply stated, it must become highly profitable to do things a better way. Making that change can be greatly assisted by the non-profits' ability to develop, test and demonstrate special case solutions. Ideas that have the most to offer may then evolve into new realities for more general and widespread application.

A sustainable future requires that we achieve an integrated understanding of the behavioral relationships between: 1) What we design and build; 2) How comprehensively we understand the role of community; 3) How we define and pursue culture; 4) The role of government;

5) Our mastery and control over technology; 6) The influence and goals of religion, and; 7) The need for environmental intelligence. The dominance of specialization has had its day and has come near bringing our civilization to its knees, just as it has with the record of civilizations that have collapsed in the past.

The cynic says, "Every generation tells itself that it has the power to solve the world's problems. Ours just happens to be the one that fell for it." The Two Worlds view is that every experience provides a lesson, an invitation and an obligation to go beyond the trials and errors of the past. In the words of an anything but simple man, Frank Lloyd Wright said simply, "We should improve on our parents. I don't think I am any better than they were but I had more opportunities."

Winston Churchill, was speaking precisely about what Frank Lloyd Wright spent a lifetime "improving on" when he said, "First we shape our environments, then they shape us." The Two Worlds focus is on the design of relationships—specifically those long-term relationships that exist between humans and nature, between technology and behavior, and between each of us and all of humanity. May what follows add to your own thoughts for a future of sustainable beauty, by design.

Vernon D. Swaback
Scottsdale Arizona

June, 2010

Vernon D. Swaback with Frank Lloyd Wright in 1957
at a Chicago television studio for a show dedicated to
Broadacre City (top); Showing Wright a drawing for
his approval outside the Taliesin West drafting room in
1958, and today in the courtyard of Swaback Partners'
Studio headquarters in Scottsdale.

THE TWO WORLDS HERITAGE

It is the relatedness and relationships of

all things that creates value.

- Frank Lloyd Wright

The "green" implications of the word "organic", now attached to farming, food, fiber, fabric, and a whole lot more, was what Frank Lloyd Wright called his architecture, starting more than seven decades before anyone used the word or understood what it meant. His entire life was an unfolding experiment, and commitment to the creative possibilities of design, and what an innovative focus on relationships, authenticity, and beauty could make possible.

Far less known or appreciated than the design of his dramatic buildings was the design of his educational and cultural live/work community known as the Taliesin Fellowship.

For the 21 years and nine months between January,

1957 and October, 1978, the community Wright created for his life and work was my home. The experience was totally unlike the more familiar pattern of having a house in one location, a job located elsewhere to pay the bills, and still other places that one might venture out to for education, entertainment and culture. For more than two decades these more typically separated "pieces" of daily life were lived out as a seamless experience of Wright's high–performance, extraordinarily beautiful and culturally–centered community.

Years later, when crusading on behalf of designing for better ways of living, my presentations would almost always be followed with developer questions like, "How can we make your ideas affordable? What do we do about codes and ordinances that demand the separation of uses and get in the way of good ideas while increasing costs?" And more recently, "How can we reduce energy and water use, and the wasteful daily, back and forth commute?"

Common to all such questions, is that the askers are most often looking for higher performing, lower cost solutions based on the individual components of a house, or a business, or a transportation system where the answers always fall short. There are abundant ways to lower the overall cost of development as well as to lower the ongoing costs for transportation, utilities and maintenance, all in the direction of becoming more sustainable, but these solutions are mainly available at the, doing more with less design of community. This requires an integration between innovative, high performing components, in one world, with an orchestration of the many needs, provisions and relationships of community in the other.

We have made reference to this being a time of transition when the world of design will be required to reach out to the design of the world. Here is how Charles Handy, an economist and professor at the London Business School, sees the present, "We are now entering the age of unreason, when the future is there to be shaped by us. A time when the only prediction that will hold true is that no predictions will hold true; a time for bold imaginings, for thinking the unthinkable, for doing the unreasonable, and for humble surrender to spirit and grace." What makes this time in history unique, is discussed further on pages 24 and 25.

It is with a focus on "this time in history" that the non-profit organization can serve a most significant role. Familiar characteristics of many non-profits that already exist include; 1) Those that provide on-going subsidies, for example, programs for low income housing; 2) Those that conduct, analyze, and publish surveys and; 3) Those based on wealth, generated in one form of expertise, applied to non-profit commitments in an entirely different area of concern.

The Two World's Community Foundation differs in all three respects; 1) Its ultimate goal is to define, test and foster prototypical non-profit examples that may lead to expanding the understanding and reach of the for-profit delivery system. This is critical because a sustainable future requires that it become both routine and profitable to do the right things. 2) For the Two Worlds quest to be considered successful it must go well beyond the arena of studies to influence and produce sustainable examples, and; 3) Unlike funding from one business, applied to entirely different pursuits, the inherent strength and mission of Two Worlds Community Foundation is a direct extension of its design-based heritage. The following five definitions and seven issues that demand our attention are presented to define and clarify what that design-based heritage is all about.

DEFINITIONS

Two Worlds: Refers to the dualities that make up our daily experiences, for example, profit and non-profit, timely and timeless, inherited and created.

Profit and Community: "I'm not saying it isn't the right thing to do, I'm just saying it won't work." This statement was made by a developer's consultant. The "right thing" referred to long term, human values, and "It won't work," referred to the developer's inability to make a profit within the period of his short-term interests.

Education: Raising the level of dialogue in order to propose and carry out programs and prototypes that broaden the definition of profit to include and center on provisions for both ecological and human values.

Educational Methods: 1) Publications to attract and inspire long-term commitments with integrated ways for measuring needs; 2) Forums that focus on individual issues and their relationships with all else; 3) Competitions and other means for studying, illustrating and proposing ecological ways of living, and; 4) Prototypical examples as the most effective form of education.

Our Inheritance: Since the beginning of urban history, every material and place fashioned into being by human dreams, ingenuity and creativity has been mined from the earth, energized by the sun and protected by the atmosphere. Future success is all about integrating values beyond those that have been acknowledged by the limited "bottom line" definitions of the past.

SEVEN ISSUES THAT DEMAND ATTENTION

The Built Environment: We are not surprised when a new subdivision or shopping center crops up that is less than a beautiful contribution to the character of the community. Mediocrity has come to look so normal that we assume anything better must be impractical.

Human Behavior: We would be stunned if the "late breaking" news announced an "outbreak" of peace, but we are not at all surprised to learn of the latest "outbreak" of violence.

Culture: We trust the technical more than the behavioral and the practical more than the artful. We tell each other, "If it seems too good to be true, it probably is." We laugh at such shop-warn sentiments as, "No one has ever gone broke underestimating the taste of the American people." We also know and say for good reason that America is the greatest nation on earth.

Governance: Our greatness began with humanity's first constitutional commitment to the sovereignty of the individual, not by birthright but sovereign by way of individual achievement. We are also aware of Socrates' warning that the eventual collapse of all democracies is caused when self-interests diminish the resources of the nation along with the resolve of those who would hold it together for the common good.

Technology: We are far better at inventing and popularizing new technologies than we are at knowing what to do with them. And we are experiencing a local to global clash between a technological revolution, changing at breakneck speed, with the glacially slow evolution of sustainable human behavior.

Religion: In addition to what we call the great religions, there are thousands of sects, but for purposes of our human future, they can all be divided into two categories; those based on personal beliefs, and those based on belonging to the group. The combined power and weakness of the latter, more often than not, includes some form of, "I am right, you are wrong." Like the concentrated power of nuclear energy, this certainty is a force that can be used to create or destroy.

Environmental Intelligence: The 21st Century's most dominant environmental quests, shared by governments, developers, corporations and non-profits alike, are carried out under the banner of being "green", with initiatives for smart growth, and sustainable development. References are also made to the need for significant changes in how we measure value, expressed in terms like the double or triple bottom line. It is easy to jump on the bandwagon of being green, in fact, it would be a rare person or group that hasn't already done so. What isn't so easy is to take serious the unmistakable implication of the need to become smart, green and sustainable as being a whole new way of life. This is far more than simply adding a gloss to what we've always done in the past. The pursuit of a higher level of environmental intelligence carriers with it an indictment of much of what we have considered to be normal in the past. Beyond the buzz words of smart, green and sustainable lies the most profound and exciting renaissance since the 15th century.

BEYOND ARGUMENT

If we had to move away from argument, what could be put in its place? The answer is exploration. Argument looks backward. Exploration and design look forward.

—Edward de Bono

The simplest definition of argument is, "I am right, you are wrong." This works best when there are agreed-upon controls for civil behavior, and where the objective is not agreement, but justice.

War, from all sides, is simply large-scale weaponized arguments where the objective is to kill or incarcerate the enemy. In all major conflicts, everyone is someone else's "enemy." Globalization, has intensified these conflicts by eliminating the historic boundaries of physical separation and limited information.

Einstein described the limitations of technology when he said, "I have no idea what weapons will be used in WWIII, but WWIV will be fought with stones and clubs." Technological advancements made to weapons used for defense, are the same as those that increase the effectiveness of attack. Battles are often "won," but this is far from true for the more fundamental on-going war.

The opposite of war, is not some form of Utopian peace. The opposite of war is the dynamic competition and co-operation of community. The reason that those who lose in the most passionately fought competitions of all kinds don't have to fight to their deaths is the same reason why Illinois doesn't launch rockets into Wisconsin. Both sides are governed by shared rules of engagement.

The Two Worlds Community replaces argument and conflict with exploration and design. It is an idea whose time has not only come, it is urgent. In making ourselves the enemies of others, we have inadvertently made ourselves the collective enemy of our planetary home. In this greatest conflict of all, our weaponry is useless, but our shared intelligence can make us partners with both nature and each other. If the 20th century has demonstrated anything, it is that the immediacy and cleverness of our technological, financial and political wizardry will always be more obviously seductive than the timeless, unifying wisdom and mystery of the universe. It is human to be clever, but without wisdom, that cleverness will more than likely be on automatic pilot to where we don't want to go.

LESS AND MORE

E.O. Wilson, one of the world's leading biologists, has placed our, not smart, not green, not sustainable" trajectory into stark focus by calculating that if all the citizens of the world were to consume the amount of resources necessary to live as we do in the United States, it would take four more planet earths. We, the now 6.7 billion inhabitants of earth have family members and friends who will be alive when another three billion people have been added to the present population, all with no increase in the earth's natural resources. To this must be added the unprecedented and accelerating increase in the world's consumption per capita.

There is no disputing that the future will be all about more, the only question is, more of what? We know there will be more people, but will this increase be accompanied by more or less of what threatens our very existence? One thing we know for certain, at least for awhile, the solution will not include adding more planets.

SEVEN CRITICAL GOALS FOR HUMANITY

- Less argument, more exploration
- More healthy ways of living, less spent on remedies
- More money and energy invested in education, less on conflict and incarceration
- More experiences to savor, less things to store or throw away
- More orchestration, less fragmentation
- More intelligence, less indulgence
- And in everything we build and do, more beauty and less discord.

Beauty is our surest indication of whether

what we do is in the most creative direction

for nature as a whole.

—Frederick Turner
The Culture of Hope

OUR WORLD OF DUALITIES

Unity is, at a minimum, two.

—Buckminster Fuller

Bucky, as he was called, never spoke without referring to this fundamental truth inherent in all of nature. Our most singular notions are in reality, the dualities that give form, energy and life to all that we experience.

The duality represented by the Foundation's logo combines our miraculous planet earth and protective atmosphere, with our own 10,000 year history of behavioral trial and error. Having now fully populated the planet while creating "God-like Technology," the 21st century question is, how will we use both our inheritance and subsequent achievements in ways that are sustainably beneficial to all, including those who are yet to be?

Love	↔	Hate
Inhaling	↔	Exhaling
Profit	↔	Non-profit
Creating	↔	Destroying
Left	↔	Right
Centrifugal	↔	Centripetal
Top	↔	Bottom
In	↔	Out
High	↔	Low
Hot	↔	Cold
Steam	↔	Ice
Peace	↔	War
Owned	↔	Shared
Man	↔	Nature
Natural	↔	Artful
Black	↔	White
Up	↔	Down
Special	↔	General
Relevant	↔	Visionary
Fragmented	↔	Integrated
Comprehensive	↔	Specific
Light	↔	Dark
Price	↔	Value
Internal	↔	External
Exploitive	↔	Sustainable
Inclusive	↔	Exclusive
Public	↔	Private
Young	↔	Old
Birth	↔	Death
Tension	↔	Compression
Male	↔	Female
Spirit	↔	Matter
Giving	↔	Receiving
Attack	↔	Defend
Power	↔	Force
Entropy	↔	Order
Technological	↔	Behavioral
Ying	↔	Yang
Rules	↔	Creativity
Science	↔	Mystery
Transactions	↔	Commitments
Timely	↔	Timeless
Facts	↔	Faith
Scheduled	↔	Eternal
Me	↔	We
Chaos	↔	Order
Weaponry	↔	Livingry
Nature	↔	Nurture
Heredity	↔	Environment

DUALITIES

Inherent in Nature

Male and female, we each have two eyes to detect depth and perspective, two ears for balance and direction and left and right brains for cognition and creativity.

Price and Value

In the world of ownership there are things money alone can buy. In the world of human values there are needs and dreams that cannot be monetized at any price.

Civilization and Culture

Like the unity of breathing in and breathing out, we see, hear, live, connect and create in the duality of our interdependence. We are the stewards and creators of our past, present and future.

The Artist

This duality comes from Albert Einstein. "The greatness of an artist lies in the building of an inner world, and in the ability to reconcile this inner world with the outer."

Nature and Development

The dramatic pre-development reconstructions on the back cover of this book are the work of the Wildlife Conservation Society showing how what is now Manhattan appeared before 1609. The comparisons illustrate the most fundamental two worlds of all, the nature we inherit and the environments we create. The 21st century demands that we move beyond arguing over preservation and development. In addition to the lands we preserve, the Two World's vision requires that we work in partnership with nature to create a sustainable, seamless magnificence between man and nature. Some will believe this to be impossible. Those on whom the future depends will regard anything less to be suicidal.

CULTURE SHIFT

Civilization is merely a way of life.

Culture is a way of making that way of life beautiful.

—**Frank Lloyd Wright**

A two worlds reality is the only kind there is, including the duality of our births and deaths. Everything we experience in between is a combination of a world of our own making and possessions with the miraculous world of photosynthesis and the breathable air that we can only share.

It is increasingly obvious that the home we can lock and call our own is becoming every day, more empowered or threatened by what we hold in common. Our experiences include both what we know and care about and that which we chose to ignore, but that is no less part of our world. Those whose view of reality is most complete, have observed that we living not only at a time of great adjustment, but also great opportunity as expressed in this two worlds view by Dee Hock, founder and Chairman Emeritus of VISA. "We are at that very point in time when a 400-year-old age is dying and another is struggling to be born—a shifting of culture, science, society, and institutions enormously greater than we have ever experienced. In the other world lies the possibility for the regeneration of individuality, liberty, community and ethics such as the world has never known, and a harmony with nature, with one another and with the divine intelligence such as the world has always dreamed."

The Jesuit priest, Teilhard de Chardin, said, "God made the world round so that one day we would have to confront each other." He also said, "The future belongs to those who can give the next generations reasons for hope." A geometric increase in population, coupled with the technology of long distance travel, first allowed us to confront each other in physical space. This was revolutionized even further when the digital world allowed us to confront each other in the 24/7 world of cyberspace.

When these new technologies are used for attack and defense, we call it war. If we use them as new tools for sustaining life, the result is community. In a one world view of argument, history would suggest that wars will always be with us, as each one paves the way for the next. A two worlds view sees the past not as prologue but as the means for making better choices in the future. We are either at the point where human evolution begins its transition away from the primitive devastation of war and toward the creation of sustainable communities or we may be on the road to a future where there is no sustainable humanity. We may want to argue about the details, but few would want to argue about which is the better direction.

James Rouse, the legendary developer of Columbia, Maryland said, "We're not coming up with the right solutions, because we're not asking the right questions." The Two World's Community Foundation is an educational forum for researching and refining the right questions in pursuit of answers that take into account the shift that Emerson had in mind when he wrote; "The slightest increase in cultural values would instantaneously revolutionize the whole of human pursuits." Without this shift, our institutions can be expected to do nothing but remain on their present trajectory toward decline.

EXPERIENTIAL EDUCATION

The title of a recent book asks, *Is the American Dream Killing You?* Another, *Last Child in the Woods*, warns of the problems associated with raising the first generation of children having no contact with nature. The American Heart Association warns that we may be raising the first generation to not outlive its parents. Obesity is increasing at a worrisome rate and according to the American Academy of Child and Adolescent Psychiatry, suicide is the third leading cause of death among 15 to 24 year-olds. These are all related to the environments that we shaped in the past, and that we can shape differently in the future. They are all matters of design, not design as style but design as a form of experiential education.

The evening news parallels the recurring message of a growing number of books with titles like *Dark Age Ahead*, by Jane Jacobs, *The Last Hours of Ancient Sunlight: The Fate of the World and What We Can Do Before It's Too Late*, by Thom Hartmann, and *Collapse: How Societies Choose to Fail or Succeed* by Jared Diamond. One of the most recent warnings by NASA's, Dr. James Hansen, carries the sobering title, *Storms of My Grandchildren: The Truth About the Coming Catastrophe and Our*

Last Chance to Save Humanity. Other "wake-up" books have more upbeat titles like, *The Answer to How is Yes: Acting on What Matters*, by Peter Block and *The Power of Design: A Force for Transforming Everything*, by Richard Farson.

If those of us alive today are to help prepare the way for a more sustainable future, we must increase our understanding of the relatedness of all things on which the success of both our individual and shared pursuits depend. The more integrated and tangible the two worlds message becomes, the more it will attract the scale of support and attention needed to achieve, in Dee Hock's words, "a harmony with nature, with one another and with the divine intelligence such as the world has always dreamed". While these words could be appreciated for their poetic character, to leave it at that would be a colossal mistake. Until and unless we can live in "harmony with nature" and "with one another," we are missing Dr. James Hansen's warning that the present represents "our last chance to save humanity."

Urgent voices are now addressing everything from the poetic to the pragmatic, and from philosophy to technology, including politics, economics and religion. The sampling of book covers on the following pages give testimony to the more integrated concern for what our individual actions are adding up to becoming.

For the first time in human history our knowledge, interest and abilities are great enough to think on a scale of interrelatedness between our personal well being and that of our shared planetary home

ONE PLANET, TWO FUTURES

We must dream of an aristocracy of achievement

arising out of a democracy of opportunity.

—Thomas Jefferson

One of the most startling truths is that those of us alive today are experiencing something that has never happened before, and will never happen again. For the first time in history, we are becoming aware of the earth's diminishing global inventory of productive soil, food, fuel and water. What we're not aware of, as explained by Robert Wright in his *Short History of Progress*, is that we are living in a "bubble". "We in the lucky countries of the West now regard our two-century bubble of freedom and affluence as normal and inevitable; it has even been called the "end" of history, in both a temporal and teleological sense. Yet this new order is an anomaly: the opposite of what usually happens as civilizations grow. Our age was bankrolled by the seizing of half a planet, extended by taking over most of the remaining half, and has been sustained by spending down new forms of natural capital, especially fossil fuels. In the New World, the West hit the biggest bonanza of all time. And there won't be another like it—not unless we find the civilized Martians of H.G. Wells, complete with the vulnerability to our germs that undid them in his War of the Worlds."

Our two possibilities are thus to continue on our present course of increasing conflict or to find better ways to partner with nature and each other. The goal of the latter requires that we create and sustain a level of community well beyond what now exists. This means overcoming the present fear-based motivations that have our institutions in decline, in order to embark on a design-based quest of a workable civilization that is yet to be.

Should we rise to the occasion, the success that can be ours for the asking holds promise beyond our wildest dreams. It is that easy and that hard. When thinking about what we hold in trust for the future, we need first acknowledge that there is a fine line between the visionary and the idea-defeating, presumption of "it won't work". Words are just words, until they become manifested in the dreams and commitments of uncommon individuals. Democracy may offer the freedom to be great, but it has always, and will always, take more than the obvious or the vote of the majority to get us there.

LEVELS OF INTENTION

The land is dotted with towns, cities, suburbs, and

the like, yet very few of these political subdivisions

are in fact communities.

—Vine Deloria, Jr.

Most of us have experienced the deadening influence of look-alike buildings and the sameness of sprawl. Why, we ask, can't we do better? The simple answer is that what we see reflects the level of intention with which it was produced. Rather than designing for long-term human values, we are surrounded with developments based on little more than the short-term demands and ease of production. Assuming that we might agree that nothing admirable has ever been achieved without commitment, see if that can be found in the following well-recognized mantras of conventional development.

- The three dominant variables for success are; location, location, and location.
- Timing is everything.
- It all comes down to velocity and margin.
- Don't make your hobby your work.
- Never fall in love with a piece of land.

The result is that we've built entire neighborhoods, cities and towns, not for life but for curb appeal, for cost per square foot, and for resale. The environments that shape our lives are so compromised by these short-term metrics that if it weren't so normal, we would judge the process far more harshly.

Early in my career, I learned, first hand, the power of intention, but in a negative direction. I had the good fortune to be planning a high profile property for an equally high profile client. I mentioned to a member of his staff that I was counting on exceptional commitment from the developer because I knew he was desirous of being a hero, only to be told; "You are right about his wanting to be a hero, but wrong about his intention. He wants to be a hero with the robber barons."

Until we are willing to accept that not everything of value can be monetized in the short term, we will continue to compromise and threaten the very future of humanity with fragmented metrics like, "it all comes down to velocity and margin." An easy way to understand and balance our two worlds view of development is to see community as being analogous to the family.

Within our families, we daily place monetary values on some things while applying commitment, love and compassion to others, and we don't seem to have a problem understanding the difference between the two. There is nothing wrong with the bottom line discipline of development, as long as we realize that the values that matter most are the human values that require a level of understanding and commitment that begins where the determinants of production and profit leave off. In addition to recognizing what can be described with words like, location, timing, velocity and margin, the two worlds view requires that we also understand and respect words like, human purpose, nurture, serve, magic, spirit and love.

*"The dreams that accompany all human actions should be **nurtured** by the places in which people live."*
—Charles W. Moore

*"I don't know what your destiny will be, but one thing I know: The only ones among you who will be really happy are those who will have sought and found how to **serve**."*
—Albert Schweitzer

*"The world is full of **magical** things, patiently waiting for our wits to grow sharper."*
—Bertrand Russell

*"The art of architecture studies structure, not only on its own terms, but the effect of structure on the **human spirit**."*
—Geoffrey Scott

*"The **best places** always make you feel like all is well with the world."*
—Andrei Codrescu

*"We must **love** our children enough to design a world which instructs them toward community, ecology, responsibility and joy."*
—David W. Orr

A HIGHER VISION

All values are human values

or else they're not valuable.

—Frank Lloyd Wright

Eventually we're going to have to connect the dots, and if we care about our children and their children it had better be sooner than later. In the process we will not only confirm the shortcomings of the standardized production of so much of what we build, we will also discover that there are places scattered all over the world that have much to teach and the lessons they represent are among those we need the most.

Such places are more varied and thus more humane, including little framed vistas and uncommon details that speak to the workmanship of someone who cared beyond the obvious. These are values that can't be measured in cost per square foot or any other numbers.

Special places like this are too varied to be categorized and perhaps too idiosyncratic to offer an easy fit with what we might find acceptable for ourselves. Most reflect an artful relationship to the land. Because they have often been built with more modest tools, the structures are designed to fit their sites, rather than first having everything bulldozed to a flat plane. The scale of such places are more based on human behavior than, for example, the technologies of engineered roadways or other one-size-fits-all infrastructure.

Among the educational activities of the Two Worlds Foundation is the locating, researching and sharing of such innovative, human scale communities, not as artifacts of the past, but as insights for doing more with less in the future. Places, for example, like Gaviotas, a South American community so amazing that it has been described as "A village to invent the world." The community has been created on land that was once one of the earth's most brutal, rain-leached savannas. Despite Columbia's political turbulence, and being located 16 hours from the nearest major city, the citizens of Gaviotas have invented windmills light enough to convert mild tropical breezes into energy, solar collectors that work in the rain, soil-free systems to raise edible medicinal crops, solar "kettles" to sterilize drinking water, and ultra-efficient pumps to tap deep aquifers and pumps so easy to operate they are hooked up to children's seesaws. The United Nations named Gaviotas a village model for the developing world.

If people starting with so little can do all this while also planting millions of Caribbean pines as a renewable crop and in the process, literally regenerating an ancient native rain forest, what should those of us who have been given so much be capable of demonstrating by what we create for ourselves and others?

Thom Hartmann writes about the creation of Salem Villages in Germany by Gottfried Müeller. Along with technical provisions that we would recognize, the settings are designed to afford a sustainable experience. "The guest house and community at Salem in Stadtsteinach is unique. Much attention has been put into the design and furnishings of the place, and into respecting the Earth's energy fields. The carpets are all natural fibers, the wiring in the walls is shielded so there is no detectable electrical radiation, and there is a thin layer of silk under each mattress to insulate people from the currents of the earth. Virtually all the food is grown in one of Salem's organic farms and a gourmet vegetarian fare is served in the guest house restaurant." Might we one day describe what we develop in such human terms, instead of, "Don't make your hobby your work, or don't fall in love with a piece of land."

In another example, the 1,500 citizens of Auroville, India, have transformed 2,500 once-barren acres into a forested garden community including on-going research and implementation for water and soil conservation, organic farming, and ecological building. Unlike so many of our new communities, for which the emphasis is on recreation and leisure, Auroville defines itself as a community of "experiential learning, fostering unity through diversity, creating a context for better community living, deepening knowledge on a broad multi-cultural level, fostering individual spiritual development and seeing learning as an on-going, open-ended process."

Auroville has more than a dozen schools including traditional village schools, Montessori-style experiential centers, as well as preparatory schools for the international baccalaureate. The Auroville commitment is to a place of unending education. The community includes a diverse mix of East, West, North and South, dedicated to deepening relationships with each other. Its cherished values are challenge, uncertainty and creativity.

Common to these examples and a good many more that the Two Worlds Community Foundation will be showcasing is that their emphasis is not on structures or things but on the high performance experience and benefit of living with a shared sense of community.

ESSENCE OF COMMUNITY

Among the most significant dualities is the expanding reach of technological power and the accelerating need for cultural commitment. Recognizing that even the most sophisticated technologies are still tools, a sustainable humanity depends on our understanding and allegiance to the behavioral essence of community. While this has no easy description, it can be clearly felt in the following observations.

We know that where **community** exists it confers upon its members' identity, a sense of belonging, and a measure of security.

—John W. Gardner

The individual is what he is, not so much in virtue of the individuality, but rather as a member of a great human **community**.

—Albert Einstein

Above all we need the reassuring presence of a visible **community**, an intimate group that enfolds us with understanding and love.

—Lewis Mumford

There can be no society without **community**. In fact there can be no life without it.

—Dee Hock

The most successful **community** would be that which contributed the most by its physical form, its institutions and its operations to the growth of people.

—James W. Rouse

We abuse the land because we regard it as a commodity belonging to us. When we see land as a **community** to which we belong, we may begin to use it with love and respect... conservation is a state of harmony between men and land.

—Aldo Leopold

As man advances in civilization, and small tribes are united into larger **communities**, the simplest reason would tell each individual that he ought to extend his social instincts and sympathies to all the members of the same nation, though personally unknown to him. This point being once reached, there is only an artificial barrier to prevent his sympathies extending to the men of all nations and races.

—Charles Darwin

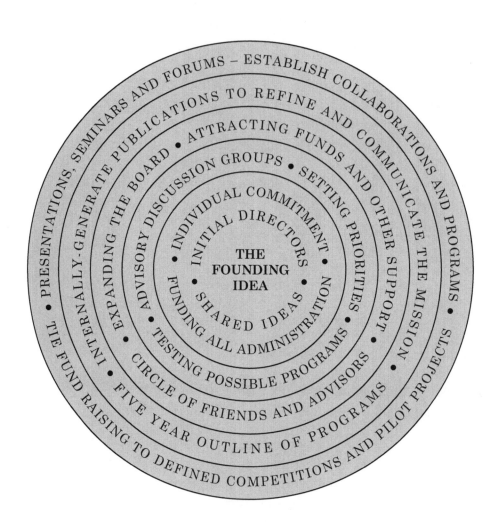

THE RADIATING LEVELS
of the
Two Worlds Community Foundation's
Outreach, Programs and Procedures

ROLE OF THE NON-PROFIT

Not everything that can be counted, counts.

And not everything that counts can be counted.

—Albert Einstein

Capitalism is far better at making things efficient, than as a discipline for creating or guaranteeing that the results will be sufficient. If this were not true, there would be little need for the non-profit world. The most nurturing and sustainable qualities of community are not to be found in the efficiency of its production methods but in the sufficiency of its provisions for daily life at all ages and stages. Community is first and foremost about human values and the relatedness of all things, including considerations for the longest horizons of time. Development has much simpler metrics, like the methods of its own processing and stylistic appeal to the general public. As for profitability, the most favorable "bottom lines" will always be those that find ways to defer as many costs as possible to other people, other places and other times. This may work for electronics and manufacturing, where technological breakthroughs can produce trajectories like Moore's law that thrives on making yesterdays achievements obsolete. But when the same laws are applied to the long-term needs of community, the results tend to produce short-term gains and long-term problems. The designed use and purpose of community is all about the complexities of privacy, sharing and longevity, all of which lie far beyond the ground rules for efficient production.

Because non-profits operate with different objectives, they have the capacity to provide not only immediate assistance to, for example, disaster relief or subsidized housing, but breakthrough solutions that, once demonstrated, can become our new, more sustainable realities. Non-profits can thus serve an important transitional role until the markets are able to take advantage of the new and demonstrated achievements.

In any area where the outputs cannot be easily measured with numbers, which includes much of human behavior, including education, health care and culture, the market is limited to measuring inputs. The result is that the cheapest methods and structures, including those for education and health are considered the most practical, at least until they cause such obvious problems that society has to pay more in remedial cost than if they were more thoughtfully considered in the first place.

Again quoting Charles Handy, one of Britain's most respected management theorists, "Anything that is unpriced is ignored by the market. The environment is the most obvious example. Air is free, so we use it and pollute it... What is not owned is not priced, and therefore cannot be included in any calculation."

What we trust to the market has less to do with intrinsic value and more to do with the structure of the market itself, including intentional manipulations that have nothing to do with the substance of the matter.

Non-profit activities are generally the reverse, in that they are positioned and motivated by a cause for which money is used to support a human purpose. As we have regrettably experienced, the markets have created financial instruments designed to serve a monetary objective, of which humans were used as a means to their own regrettable end. This dilemma was summarized by Philippe Meyer, a former Wall Street trader, saying, "If running the economy off the cliff makes you money, you will do it, and you will do it every day of the week."

CREATING VALUE

We too easily think of resources as a shrinking pie, representing a fixed value that can either be divided into ever smaller pieces, or altogether hoarded by some to the exclusion of the rest. Frederick Turner is among those who see a far more creative view of value. "In agreement with many fields of twentieth-century natural science, ranging from evolutionary theory to chaos theory," he believes that, "value is continually created by the natural universe... and that human beings can share in and accelerate its growth." While he views our market system of capitalist economics as the best system yet devised for exchange, he nonetheless regards its present state to be, "a linear and clumsy attempt to imitate the more subtle processes of true value-creation." For purposes of our need to do a better job in how we plan for a sustainable human future, the Two Worlds Community Foundation values the non-profit world of exploration as an important proving ground for doing things a better way.

EDUCATIONAL PROGRAMS

The Foundation's mission is carried out in four dominant areas, each designed to support and amplify the others. The first is the writing and publication of white papers and books, along with corresponding lectures that explore, establish and articulate the Foundation's educational purpose and insights. The second consists of Forums and Seminars, individually designed and hosted by the Foundation and occurring in a diversity of locations. The third are educational competitions, designed to research, illustrate and broadcast, "doing-more-with-less" solutions for the programming and design of community. The programs are designed to address innovations that are not now achievable by way of the profit-centered marketplace, but could one day become the new norm. The fourth consists of physical pilot projects, used as living demonstrations for more efficient, less costly, and more sustainable ways of living in tune with nature and each other.

The structure and purpose of all programs are informed and guided by the Foundation's design and education-based heritage of analogous experience as referenced along with the following descriptions for each educational category.

PUBLICATIONS

This *Two Worlds Handbook* is the Foundation's second publication. The first was, *Living in Two Worlds, The Creative Path to Community*. The Foundation's publication heritage includes a related stream of articles and white papers, including *Designing the Future*, a book funded by the Arizona State University Foundation and published in 1997 by ASU's Herberger Center for Design Excellence. As an example of the public purpose of the Foundation's heritage, *The Creative Community: Designing for Life* published in 2003, prompted a worldwide response. Anthony Downs, Senior Fellow with The Brookings Institution wrote, "*The Creative Community* presents credible and reasoned arguments supported by a stunning collection of drawings and photographs. Leaders in all cities and regions now grappling with how to influence the futures of their communities will surely profit from this book."

Designing with Nature, published in 2005 was followed by *Creating Value: Smart Development and Green Design*, a national, award-winning book on sustainable design, published in 2007 and distributed globally by the non-profit Urban Land Institute. This was followed in 2009 by *Believing in Beauty*.

VISIONING FORUMS

The Forums are dialogue-based sessions designed around their respective sponsor's interests and held wherever that interest emerges or is the most effective location relating to the subject matter. Participants are selected in keeping with the program's objectives. Manuals are prepared including biographies of each participant as well as positioning narratives and related materials designed as an inspirational base for the one or two-day conferences. In addition to the handbooks, there are always a series of image boards, and power point materials prepared in advance to facilitate and empower the Forum's purpose.

A professional writer chronicles the proceedings for distribution to the participants and may be the basis for one or more related publications. The extent to which the event is allowed to be attended by an outside audience or the press is determined by the sponsor's objectives.

The Foundation's heritage in this area includes municipal visioning programs that have extended for a few days up to a few years. As an example, a two day session called the "Karakahl Forum", was convened on January 18 and 19, 2000 to discuss the dualities and relationships of a wide variety of community-related issues represented by its diversity of participants (see pages 77-99).

Among the presenters were; Richard Bowers and Sam Campana, Scottsdale's City Manager and Mayor; Richard Daley, the Executive Director of the Arizona-Sonora Desert Museum; Max De Pree, Chairman emeritus, Herman Miller, Inc. and member of *Fortune* magazine's business Hall of Fame; Gloria Feldt, national president of Planned Parenthood; Pam Hait, award-winning author and journalist; Carl Hodges, founding Director of the University of Arizona's Environmental Research Laboratory and atmospheric physicist who pioneered the production of alternative fuels; George Land, general systems scientist, author of *Grow or Die* and consultant to Fortune 500 companies; Rev. Culver H. Nelson, founder and 50-year senior minister of Church of the Beatitudes which was the nation's fastest growing United Church of Christ; Dr. James Schamadan, CEO of Scottsdale

Health Systems and specialist in both covert military strategies and for the handling of explosive ordinance and hazardous/radioactive chemicals; Lynne Twist who has raised $100's of millions for a global range of ending hunger projects, preservation of the world's rain forests, and the emergence of women, and; Steve Wilson, journalist, editor, Peace Corps volunteer in the Palau Islands of Micronesia and professor at the Walter Cronkite School of Journalism at Arizona State University. The titles for each participant relates to their positions at the time of the Forum. Sample statements from each, along with representative materials from the Karakahl Forum are included in the Appendix.

Another seminar, held on March 11, 2003 under the banner of "The Two Worlds Forum," is described on pages 5-10 and 126-147, in *Living in Two Worlds, The Creative Path to Community.*

Confirmed by the experience of prior gatherings, the most effective individuals are those with the following characteristics;

- A personal interest and commitment, beyond any formal job description with respect to the announced topics to be discussed.
- Individuals who express themselves in ways that inspire a deeper exploration from the group as a whole.
- Persons who define their own work and interests in ways that extend beyond any one or more specific professions.
- Those who explore relationships and solutions in ways that others may regard to be unwise, impractical, or even impossible.
- Individuals who are successful, but for purposes of the Forum, what is valued most is their desire to explore well beyond the specifics of their past.

Details

Two weeks before the event, each participant furnishes a brief statement of their interests and knowledge, along with a biography, and one or more related items to be shared, which may include articles, cartoons, charts and statistics.

One week prior to the event, these materials are assembled into binders and shipped to the participants.

Wherever possible, the Forum meeting places are ones with special charm and, weather permitting, operable windows and nearby gardens.

COMPETITIONS

While there may be occasions where juried competitions result in the winner being awarded a related commission, because the competitions are for educational purposes, the more typical programs are those in which the selected winner receives a cash prize.

No two competitions are ever the same. The educational objective shared by all is to research, design, illustrate and evaluate programs that go beyond the reach of what the present conventional market believes to be feasible. To achieve more wide-spread educational benefit, where appropriate, the programs are published with the findings of each competition treated as public events.

The competition programs go beyond the physical to describe the human, purpose-driven objectives of each assignment. The more closely the programs can relate to complex, daily, user-centered effectiveness, as opposed to creating iconic artifacts, the greater the focus can be on what performs in the most strategic manner for its human purpose. This is an entirely different pursuit than looking for something which may "perform" at its best as an image on a post card. Jurors are selected based on their credentials and experience related to each competition.

A key outreach of each competition includes presentation to developers, community groups and professional societies of all kinds. A wide variety of programs are designed with each one addressing one or more educational aspects of community.

Frank Lloyd Wright was often asked how it felt to be, "so far ahead of his time." He objected to the question saying, "The time for an idea to happen is as soon as someone has it and the ability to carry it out," which leads to the next level of the Foundation's educational purpose.

PILOT PROJECTS

Whether the focus is on a single system, one or more structures, or small to large versions of community, applicants seeking the Foundation's support for their proposed pilot projects must submit: 1) Full, clear and compelling presentations of the concept; 2) Written materials, stating the pilot project's purpose and length of time required to carry out the demonstration; 3) How it will be monitored, and; 4) Confirmation of the applicant's ability to manage the full intent of the program.

As long as they are compatible with the Foundation's, 501 (c) 3 status, the Foundation will consider any form of short or long term partnerships or collaborations that further its educational mission to explore, communicate and demonstrate sustainable relationships between humanity and nature and humanity with itself.

The Beauty Principle

Buckminster Fuller, the great scientist/inventor/designer, said he never designed for beauty, but if what he was working on, didn't turn out to be beautiful, he knew he had made a mistake. Scientist speak of the "beauty principal." If two conflicting, but equally plausible theories emerge as answers to a given study, the one that is most coherent and most beautiful, is regarded to be the right solution. When what we design is both functional and beautiful, it is most like the fully integrated ecosystems services of nature.

Buckminster Fuller's geodesic sphere for the United States Pavilion at the Expo '67 World's Fair in Montreal

PUTTING IT ALL TOGETHER

"The future is always unknown and unknowable."

–Arthur C. Clarke

The Foundation's educational programs include the design and administration of competitions that explore and illustrate beneficial patterns for ways of living in the here and now conceived in ways that are likely to continue working well into the future. As for anyone's ability to predict the future, we agree with Herman Kahn, an acknowledged futurist and founder of the Hudson Institute. "Most descriptions of the future, if read very carefully, read more like accurate descriptions of the present."

With this observation in mind, the Foundation's philosophy is that the best way to know the future, is to create a better way of doing things in the present. This involves giving new expression to the timeless relationships between, man and nature, old and young, life and work, spirit and matter, place, proximity and purpose.

It includes all the obvious objectives of reducing the use of water and energy, recycling wastes, eliminating or reducing the daily commute, and other ecological considerations. It views the ways and means of the overall community as being as much or more about education as is the classroom. Respect and dignity are more the consequences of genuine relationships than learned mannerisms. Work and study are not simply means to an end, rather, like breathing in and breathing out, work and study are related fundamentals of life. The same is true for what we too easily isolate as the arts and culture. Our most important work of art must one day include communities as our full-scale expressions of the art of living.

Summary of Behavior and Design

- Individual and community behavior is humanity's greatest and only ultimate strength, for which technology is but a tool. We too easily submit to believing it to be the other way around.

- The historic record is that advancements in technology, from humans walking on the moon to genomics in the laboratory, are rapid to the point of disbelief, while advancements in human behavior are both fragile and slow.

- Non-governmental organizations (NGO's) are increasingly important because, like nature, they exist outside the realm of both dictatorial power and election cycles.

- Non-profit organizations are increasingly needed because it is easier and more tempting for profit-making enterprises to be efficient within their own measures, than sufficient in terms beyond their immediate interests.

- The most thoughtful physical environments are those that encourage and inspire positive relationships between individuals and nature. Design is the shaper of both our personal and shared experiences.

- Because of our growing human dominance, we are moving from the world of design to the design of the world.

- The opposite of war is not the power to enforce peace with military might, but to design, inspire and create a sustainable global community.

- Design is the fundamental integration between the nature we inherit, the technology we invent, and the behaviors we practice.

- Design is the rudder of culture, marshalling the use of the earth's resources and creating beauty in the physical environment, while helping to shape the meaning of life.

- Visions and dreams are the unquenchable energy for translating dreams into action. Development is humanity's means for translating actions into new realities.

"When we try to pick anything out by itself, we find

it hitched to everything else in the Universe.

No particle is ever wasted or worn out, but

eternally flowing from use to use."

–John Muir

The educational purpose of the Two Worlds Community Foundation is to explore and communicate the relationships between human values, as portrayed in these photos with the positive influences of what we design in concert with nature.

DESIGNING THE FUTURE

None of us lives at the point where the Creation be-

gan. But every one of us lives at a point where the

Creation continues.

—Scott Russell Sanders

Remember the developers mantras quoted on page 27—"Don't fall in love with a piece of land, don't make your hobby your work, and location and timing are everything"? This is sound advice, as long as whatever is being developed is a tactical means to a financial end. But what happens when the piece of land we're ultimately developing is called "planet earth"? Wouldn't that make it somewhat more difficult to distinguish what it takes to make a profit, from what it takes to create a sustainable and fulfilling way of life?

And how are we to think about, "It all comes down to velocity and margin"? What if we are engaged in pursuits for which we care and love, do we really want to treat it as nothing more than what we buy and sell? And if margin means profit, isn't that a quality we want to experience in everything we experience?

All of this brings us to the developer's well known pursuit of "The Big Idea." Whatever else it may mean, the marketing search for the Big Idea is generally focused on a single question. How can we interest buyers in what we have to offer? It is a perfectly reasonable and even essential question for many transactions, but it too easily tends towards both the superficial and the unsustainable. For example, according to *The Weight of Nations: Material Outflows from Industrial Economics*, one half to three quarters of the annual resource inputs to industrialized economies are returned to the environment as wastes within a year.

When it comes to how we shape our lives in pursuit of community, the really big ideas are all based on human values that might be considered a culture of relationships. Culture was defined by Frank Lloyd Wright as a way of making civilization beautiful. Beauty was defined by the poet Keats as "truth." Einstein agreed, so did Buckminster Fuller. After having tried all the easier to master technologies, we will rediscover that the sustainable society is one which is more in league with the timeless truths of beauty, than the "timing is everything" domains of sales and marketing.

That which technology has often done best is to correct problems associated with earlier technologies that created the problems in the first place. Have the amazing advances in digital weaponry, all created since the typewriter and carbon copy era of the Second World War, made civilization more sustainable? Not only is the answer no, such advancements haven't even contributed to the effectiveness of war.

LEARNING FROM TRAJECTORIES

While the technological advances in the weaponry used today would appear to be nothing short of magical to warriors of the past, there have been no such advances in our corresponding behaviors. If our understanding of such diverse subjects as war and biology were limited to teachable moments in the classroom, we might feel that we've made great progress. However with a more holistic understanding of the trajectories of where we've been and where we're heading, scientists warn us that we are causing a biological holocaust that is destroying life ten thousand times more rapidly than the natural rate of extinction.

While the technological advances for the discovery and extraction of oil have been impressive, again in terms of trajectory, in less than a single generation, China's needs alone will exceed the current total world's production by 13 million barrels a day.

We depend on rich soil to grow the food we need for survival. In spite of there being entire agencies, industries, and university departments focused on this critical resource, we lose 100 million acres of farmland and 24 billion tons of topsoil, resulting in 15 million acres of new desert every year.

We have created unprecedented technologies for microfiltration and other means for the reuse of water yet much of the water we use comes from large underground aquifers that date back to many ice ages ago. When this ancient resource is used up, we will have to live mainly off rainwater, which returns far less than we now use. There will be wars over water.

To move in the direction of a sustainable future demands a whole new way of seeing. With this broader perspective, architects like Frank Lloyd Wright will be understood to have represented a deeply felt sense of science, just as Einstein's science will be increasingly understood to be a work of art. We will at long last awaken to the realization that nature has no separate departments for art and science, nor for profit and non-profit. Everything is related, and all are matters of design in the highest and finest sense of the word.

The educational role of the Two World's Community Foundation is to identify and shape special case examples into visible guides for greater application by others. It is time for what we call "love" to flood our spiritual relationships with life, with the land, and with each other. If these words sound just a bit too poetic to have meaning in the real world, then God help us if we think the real world can get along without love.

The outer circles portray our two choices; To live in balance with nature, or to edge ever-closer to ecological collapse. The three overlapping circles in the center are what NASA's Dennis Bushnell calls, "the triangle of conflict" between food, fuel and water. In the simplest of terms, our two choices are the lose-lose of increasing conflict, or the win-win of creating community.

SUSTAINABILITY REQUIRES PASSION

The city of Chicago put it's power behind the building of Cabrini Green, St. Louis did the same with Pruit Igoe. It might be assumed that those responsible for the design of such massive projects took their job far too seriously to describe it with soft-sounding words like love and beauty. No doubt more clearly defined procedures with multiple checkpoints along the way were followed with great care. The structures were built, occupied, and the efforts celebrated. But success takes more than mastering the cold hard facts of economics and construction. The projects were so bereft of human values that they both had to be entirely demolished.

THREE WHO FELL IN LOVE

George Washington fell in love with a piece of land and created the sustainable inspiration of Mt. Vernon. For a period of 45 years from 1754 until his death in 1799, the multiple buildings and gardens of Mt. Vernon were the spiritual home of its founder and the father of this country. It is impossible to consider Washington's life independent of Mt. Vernon. It served as his touchstone, always there to empower his career as military leader and later, president. Even during the years when he had to be away, Mt. Vernon remained "home" in his thoughts. It represented an authentic relationship to the beauty of place, adding richness to his life.

Thomas Jefferson fell in love with a piece of land and created Monticello. Like Mt. Vernon, Jefferson's design of Monticello is more a genuine feature of its setting than anything to do with the pretense of extravagance. Monticello is inventive, even experimental, including 40 years of changes, as Jefferson pursued his passion for design.

My mentor fell in love with every piece of land he ever designed for, including the creation of his own Taliesin and Taliesin West. In Arizona he said, "We have met the desert, loved it and made it our own." He spoke of the simple beauty of south central Wisconsin where Taliesin is located, with the poetic sense of a lover.

For the future, the path to success will be increasingly dependent on the integrating insights and energy of our highest levels of commitment and intention. We will come to see comprehensive design as humanity's global positioning system for knowing where we are in order to provide directions for where we want and need to be. In this pursuit, the educational role of the Two Worlds Community Foundation is to research and nurture special case, non-profit, studies all in directions that are both beneficial and sustainable. Each in our own way, our individual and shared purpose is to become partners in creating the future, wherever that may lead. The stakes for humanity have never been higher, never more global, never more threatening and never more promising.

THE ULTIMATE GARDEN

Broadacre City is certainly the most American scheme ever devised for our built environment, yet even today... it remains an enigma to most laymen.

—H. Allen Brooks

Eight decades have passed since Frank Lloyd Wright first designed, described and illustrated what he called Broadacre City. It was his concept for a city that would one day "be everywhere and nowhere," based on the idea that decentralization would lead to the creation of new forms of multi-centered communities. Four of Wright's 14 books, including *The Disappearing City* (1932), *When Democracy Builds* (1945), *The Living City* (1958), and *The Industrial Revolution Runs Away* (1969), were dedicated to giving this new pattern of decentralized development an ordered, artful form. In addition to innovative building types and complex integration, Wright's comprehensive approach included the architectural design of roads, freeways, bridges, and all other aspects of the built environment that would be affected by the growing dominance of personal mobility. For Wright, these were all matters for design.

How clear was his vision?

More than three-quarters of a century after Wright wrote *The Disappearing City*, Richard Ingersoll, in his well-researched book, *Sprawltown*, offered this answer, "Almost without notice the city has disappeared." Ingersoll goes on to say, "Though people continue to live in places with names like Rome, Paris, New York, and Beijing, the majority of the inhabitants of the developed world live in urban conditions somewhere outside the center city."

To what extent is everything a matter for design?

Insights surrounding this question now fill a growing number of books, with one of the most recent being, Richard Farson's *The Power of Design: A Force for Transforming Everything*. "Design may soon become the byword of leadership and management. Because of the growing recognition of design's power to affect human behavior, increasing numbers of organization specialists think executives should adopt a design perspective. Management guru Tom Peters says it flatly: "Everything is design.""

An idea whose time has come

For scholars who have praised Wright's architecture it has been more the rule than the exception to ignore or demean his crusading on behalf of a new form of city. Not only is Wright's concept for Broadacre City the least-understood area of his work, it is frequently dismissed by urban scholars as a regrettably accurate vision for what we now decry as single-use sprawl.

This is surely puzzling considering that his well-documented concept includes a seamless integration of single-family residences, attached houses, including those over shops and industry, mid-rise buildings combining residential and office uses on the same levels, and with ground-floor retail. He also included special-case provisions, for example, residential and farm uses under the same roof. Broadacre provided extensive civic environments, including government centers, airports, stadiums, sports venues, inns, cultural parks, and a variety of innovative market centers that didn't exist at the time but are becoming familiar in the present.

As portrayed in Wright's integrated concept, we are only now beginning to think of housing, transportation, food production, and an abundant supply of clean air and water as highly coordinated, self-generating systems. With his organic architecture, the world's most celebrated architect set the tone for what we now call smart, green, and sustainable, saying "It is quite impossible to consider the building as one thing, its furnishings as another, and its setting and environment, still another."

Rather than choosing up sides, between being for or against whatever one understands or believes to be true about Broadacre City, two observations are beyond argument. The first is that Wright's vision was not only accurate, he also demonstrated how to take advantage of the decentralizing influences of technology. The second is that we missed an opportunity to give that new thrust the benefit of a comprehensive and artful urban form. We also missed what Wright was demonstrating about the benefits of community by way of his own daily life and work as an integral part of the Taliesin Fellowship.

The Taliesin Equivalent

In the briefest possible terms, life at Taliesin was a microcosm of community in which, work, life, education, culture, entertainment, health and well-being, localized food production, minimal water and energy use, learning by doing, eliminating the daily back and forth commute between home and work, having daily dialogue with individuals from all over the world, and living in tune with the lessons of nature, all took place as an intensely seamless experience. No one closely associated with the Taliesin Fellowship would seriously suggest that it be replicated, but its lessons for adaptive application include insights far greater than anything to be found in the host of textbooks on urban planning.

In the fall of 1958, in the Hillside living room at Taliesin in Wisconsin, Wright concluded his Sunday breakfast talk saying, "It's time for us to pack up and make our move to the desert. We're leaving here with our work half done. I'll probably die with my work half done." That moment came just five months later on April 9, 1959.

Hundreds of books have been written about Frank Lloyd Wright's life and work. The last of the books he wrote himself, was titled, *A Testament*. For its dedication he chose a single sentence from Alfred Lord Tennyson, "Most may raise the flowers now, for all have got the seeds." The one, greatest collection of flowers that remains to be raised - that which is to be humanity's most significant achievement, is the artful, sustainable, high performance community. Among all who now have the seeds, may there be those who will forever commit to plant and care for this greatest garden of all.

Frank Lloyd Wright in 1935, working on the model for his concept of Broadacre City

A SCREAM FROM THE HEART

To witness someone saying, "I'm a realist!" invites no inquiry. It is as though we all know and have accepted what it means to be "real" as something equivalent to the force of gravity pulling us in the same direction without the need for effort on our part.

I've come to see anyone who counters whatever is being suggested by saying, "I'm a realist," as simply confessing to being a non-participant – someone with nothing to offer other than to add their weight, not to the real but to the "obvious." The reward of being obvious is to exist in a realm that requires no burden of proof.

The difference between the "real" and the "obvious," is that the obvious is seldom real, and the real is almost never obvious. For example, we might easily agree that there is nothing obvious about the "real" creative works of our greatest artists or the very real discoveries of our most brilliant scientists. Also, the fact that we can all feel the obvious pull of gravity does nothing to limit the very "real" opportunity for heavier than air flight or the advent of human-launched satellites. In like manner, the fear that fuels the devastation of war, could just as well be used as a springboard to inspire an all-out quest for the wealth-creating blessings of community.

The notion that there may be something of value beyond the obvious is an old message that is beginning to be heard in new ways. It is a more inclusive, global version of Winston Churchill's observation that, "Americans can always be counted on to do exactly the right thing just as soon as they've tried and exhausted every other possibility."

When it comes to looking for ways to make the world work, we have not yet, it seems, "exhausted all other possibilities." For example, given our present mind-set, what could seem less real, inspire more backlash, and require more scrutiny, than suggesting a fearless vision for a future in harmony with nature that works for all of humanity? This would surely be suspect, if for no other reason than that it would challenge our most readily shared and obvious tendency towards fear.

What the gravitational pull is to our physical world, fear is to the world of our emotions. And like gravity, which is a limiting force that makes our physical world possible, fear is a limiting force, that makes our emotional and spiritual world essential. Just as finding our right relationship with gravity is the source and measure of our physical strength, doing the same with fear can be the source and measure of what makes us human.

Gravity and fear are no less real in the 21st century than they were in the cave. We've simply had more trial and error experiences to expand our understanding. But while we've overcome the obvious limitations of gravity, where fear is concerned we've simply replaced our earliest threats with ever-greater ones of our own making. According to E.O. Wilson, the result is that "We have created a real mess. In order to avoid wrecking our planetary home, we have to settle down and together devise the means to achieve sustainable development while preserving our biosphere," Wilson continues, "The good news is that the same thinking that has gotten us into trouble – those brains of ours – can get us out. We're smart. We can do it."

Leading by Design

The "we" that Wilson refers to as those who "can do it," are neither the "realists" nor those who have dominated the decision-making of the past with their oratorical skills for winning arguments. During the 20th century, it was most common for high officials to be largely those who were trained in the law. It was thought reasonable that anyone trusted to make major decisions affecting everything from health care to international policy should have more generally recognized and provable credentials. By comparison, artists, philosophers, visionaries, and dreamers of all kinds have been thought of as specialty providers, less prepared for serious decision-making.

Buckminster Fuller prophesized a new kind of design-based leader as a "synthesis of artist, inventor, mechanic, objective economist, and evolutionary strategist." The emergence of this new leadership is now in our midst, including individuals who are creating more efficient buildings, more integrated land-use patterns, the restoration of once degraded ecologies, scientists who are applying nature's methods for health and healing, and all others who are discovering greater insights for living in balance with our earthly home.

We have arrived at a point where we must decide whether to continue with our patterns of exploitive fragmentation or to transition our energies in ways that favor ecologically competent design. We have reached the pinnacle of what our old ways of seeing can produce. The good news is that our vision has never been greater, our tools never so amazing, and our understanding of both nature and each other has reached an intensity that offers the unprecedented clarity of choosing between mutual annihilation or co-creative exploration.

While a sustainably beautiful future is ours for the asking, we cannot expect it to force itself on us against our will. It's time to recognize that to continue from this point forward with what worked as part of a frontier ethic, would be nothing short of disastrous.

In 2003, Jennifer Verrall, a journalist with *The Age* newspaper in Victoria, Australia referred to my book, the *Creative Community, Designing for Life*, "as a scream from the heart against the horrors of 20th and 21st century urban sprawl and a plea for sensibility to be brought into the equation." The Two World's Community Foundation has been created to amplify that scream and to intensify the pursuit of sensibility.

The visionary view is simply a willing ability to understand each moment in terms of its trajectory. All points in time carry evidence of both their historic past and likely future. While this has always been so, what gives unprecedented urgency to the present is that we, the more than six billion, heading toward nine billion citizens of earth, combined with the unprecedented state of our technology, has not only placed us in global contact and conflict with each other, but collectively, we are in global conflict with the planetary resources of life.

A New Way of Seeing

While we continue to place our greatest technologies, strategies and treasure in the service of the attack and defense of war, we are beginning to understand that we can no longer hold out any reasonable hope of being able to fight our way to victory, at least not in the ways of the past. Among the reasons that place us on the threshold of unprecedented success is that we are losing patience with the old way of seeing. Here in brief is how and why the best for humanity is yet to be.

By trial and error, we are beginning to distinguish between the good and productive battles, from those that produce nothing but losses for everyone. We are becoming less willing to support the self-defeating fighting that produces little more than death and destruction. Our daily news serves up unrelenting images of carnage resulting from each side fighting to defend it's deepest beliefs.

The good fights are those we wage within ourselves, in pursuit of understanding what works and what doesn't. All great achievements, including the paintings, sculpture, music, dance, literature, science, and laws that live on, reflect the creative battles that individuals wage within themselves. We are beginning to understand that what we have called "art," rather than being a human specialty is a human necessity. The greatest works of art are not limited to the special features that hang on a gallery wall or get performed on a stage. If humanity is to have a future, it will be because we have found ways to create artful relationships with each other as well as our collective relationships with the environments we share.

Without this understanding, the greater our fragmented accomplishments become, the more we threaten our very existence. To understand why this is so, consider what tactical and engineering brilliance it took to make possible the horrors of 9/11. Think of the engineering research and extraordinary feats of construction that were necessary for there to be an oil spill capable of destroying the livelihood of generations and the ecology of both sea and land. Think of the computerized power and algorithmic calculating that it took on May 6, 2010 for there to be a thousand-point drop in the Dow Jones Industrials, 700 of which occurred in less then half an hour, including buy and sell orders made within 15 millionths of a second, all with neither initial warning nor later explanation. These three very different examples of destruction have one thing in common. They would have been impossible without the human brilliance that created our unprecedented reach of technology.

Lessons for the Future

What can we learn from the past that has the most to offer our quest for a sustainable future? The first is that there are no easy answers and little room for those who consider themselves "realists." Because the sustainable community is among humanity's greatest achievements, expect it to be not only rewarding to experience but difficult to achieve.

The second lesson is to place all technology and accounting in the service of human values. That we have for so long had this the other way around now threatens all we hold dear. No matter what other opinions appear to exist, we may all agree that there is nothing practical, attractive, or profitable about human extinction.

The third is to acknowledge that words like, proportion, beauty, relationships, care, quality, and community, however soft they may have sounded in the past, now carry far more hope for the future than what we have considered to be the more substantial notions of function, location, margin, and the most fragmented and manipulated measure of all, the so-called bottom line – for whom, and for how long?

We conclude this cry from the heart with five observations that bear repeating:

- An artist/architect like Frank Lloyd Wright will be understood to have represented a deeply felt sense of science, just as Einstein's science will be increasingly understood to be a work of art.

- It is time for what we call "love" to flood our spiritual relationships with the land, with life, and with each other.

- We will come to see comprehensive design as humanity's global positioning system for knowing where we are in order to provide directions for where we want and need to be.

- Each in our own way, our individual and shared purpose is to become partners in creating a sustainable future.

- The stakes for humanity have never been greater, never more global, never more threatening and never more promising.

APPENDIX

- QUESTIONS AND ANSWERS
- KARAKAHL FORUM
- PRODUCTION DWELLINGS
- THE GOVERNING BOARD
- IRS FORM 1023 EXCERPTS

QUESTIONS AND ANSWERS

1. Wouldn't the Foundation's mission be easier to understand if it focused on more specific issues?

The focus is on specific issues, including alternative fuels, water conservation, transportation, land use, multi-purpose accessibility, education, arts and culture, governance, codes and ordinances, as well as environmental and spatial influences on behavior. However, the study of the pieces are subsets that are only given meaning and value in the context of their beneficially-designed relationships. The need to go beyond the pieces, is expressed in ecological terms by the Pulitzer Prize-winning biologist, E.O. Wilson.

"An ecologist sees the whole as a network of energy and material continuously flowing into the community from the surrounding physical environment, and back out, and then on. This is the continuity on which our own existence depends."

2. I understand why the Foundation's purpose requires, educating and illustrating, but isn't it going too far for a non-profit to involve itself in the creation of pilot projects?

The record suggests that information by itself is an inadequate motivator. Humanity has demonstrated its inability to learn anything of positive environmental benefit, without being able to experience some level of demonstration. Einstein, among others, has pointed out that, "Setting an example is not the main means of influencing others, it is the only means."

3. The Foundation's literature suggests that new technologies should not be expected to be the main source for achieving a sustainable world. Isn't this view inconsistent with the technological quest for wind, solar, biofuels and other non-polluting sources of alternative energy?

Technology can be amazing to the point of seeming miraculous. Heavier-than-water ships can float, heavier-than-air planes can fly, and we routinely convey written, spoken and visual information around the world, at the speed of light. The computing power that once took entire buildings to house, we now manipulate in the palm of our hands. However, as seen from the two worlds view, we observe that the same technology that made it possible to build, occupy, and operate New York's Twin Towers as a center for world trade, also made possible the death and destruction of 9/11. It is futile to look for easy-to-achieve technological advances to save us from ourselves. A sustainable future for humanity will be at least 75 percent, if not a whole lot more, dependent on the heart-centered, behavioral relationships of humanity. Václav Havel stated it most clearly. "The salvation of this human world lies nowhere else than in the human heart, in the human power to reflect, in human meekness and human responsibility. Without a global resolution in human consciousness nothing will change for the better and the catastrophe towards which this world is headed will be unavoidable."

4. **Malcomb Forbes, the wealthy capitalist crusader had a different message. "What is the answer to 99 out of a hundred questions? Money." How is this answer seen from the "Two Worlds" perspective?**

Forbes' answer is true for any needs that can be satisfied by what money alone can buy. Providing environmentally sustainable conditions for a sustainable humanity, may take a lot of money, but money alone won't do it. The reason is simple. The heart and soul of the sustainable community is all about mastering the complexity of relationships, including both the relationships of physical design and those confronted in human behavior.

5. **The Foundation's publication *Living in Two Worlds, The Creative Path to Community* states that the future depends on applying insights from the world of design to the design of the world. Isn't this a bit arrogant?**

Only if you aren't aware that as humans, we are already "designing" the world, but rather than doing so with holistic commitment, we are destroying it by default. James Martin is an acknowledged expert on the social and economic impact of computers and technology. In his latest book, *The Meaning of the 21st Century, a Vital Blueprint for Ensuring our Future,* he writes, "The 21st Century is an extraordinary time - a century of extremes. We could create much grander civilizations, or we could trigger a new Dark Ages... Evolution on Earth has been in nature's hands. Now, suddenly, it is largely in human hands."

Many others, like Michael Pollan are coming to similar conclusions. "Partly by default, partly by design, all of nature is now in the process of being domesticated... even the wild now depends on civilization for its survival."

6. What is meant by the assertion that the Two Worlds approach is a replacement for argument?

With all of humanity being interconnected and interdependent, both with itself and the resources of earth, arguments in the form of "I am right, you are wrong" have become both ineffective and dangerous. To live, think and feel in "Two Worlds" terms is to replace "either/or" arguments with "both/and" explorations.

7. Among the Two Worlds ideas is that the opposite of war is not peace, instead the opposite of war is community. What does that mean?

War is the militarized version of "I am right, you are wrong." The hope of both sides is to be victorious over the other. This is both costly, deadly and unsustainable as a way of life, and offers nothing but diminishing returns for all. The opposite of war and the only sustainable hope for humanity is to achieve the creative relationships of community.

THE KARAKAHL FORUM

The structure of the Foundation's Visioning Forums is outlined on pages 41-44. The following is a glimpse into the forum's more human and widely varied experiences including excerpts from statements presented by the participants. The titles provided with each name are what they were at the time of the Forum.

Steve M. Wilson, Journalist

The central premise of the forum, is that the level of dialogue about our community's future needs elevating, and once lifted, it is likely to lead to a better outcome. I agree with the need. Discussions about growth and development are routinely obstructed by self-interest, stereotyping, short-term vision and black-and-white thinking. If people can communicate more clearly, open their minds and consider new ideas, it seems reasonable to expect better results.

I hope Daniel Yankelovich, the social scientist and public-opinion expert, is right. In his new book, *The Magic of Dialogue: Transforming Conflict into Cooperation*, he writes, "when dialogue is done skillfully, the results can be extraordinary" and describes encouraging examples.

"Dialogue is the opposite of debate. The purpose of debate is to win an argument, to vanquish an opponent. Dialogue has very different purposes. It would be inconceivable to say that someone 'won' or 'lost' a dialogue. In dialogue, all participants win or lose together. They have come to see that the worst possible way to advance mutual understanding is to win debating points at the expense of others."

Brent E. Herrington, Visionary Developer

For many of us, the most formative, most life-shaping experiences of childhood were completely intertwined with the neighborhood or community our family was part of. This includes the neighbors we knew, the friends we made, the pets we adopted, the churches we attended, the paths we walked and the trees we climbed, the prejudices we endured, the behavior of adults we admired, the adventures we shared, the scandals we heard whispered about, the teachers we loved and feared, the dares we took, the bullying we gave and received on our way to learning compassion, the contests we won and lost, the chores we performed, the small treasures we coveted from the neighborhood stores... these were the experiences that shaped our beliefs, colored our perceptions and defined our character. By extension, these experiences, common to many of us, provide the underpinnings for the cultural values and civic standards that bind us together.

Most of our country's civic capacity is generated at the community level, including virtually all of the important social, civic, cultural, spiritual, artistic, recreational and educational institutions that give strength and substance to our society. Families are the building blocks of our communities and communities are the building blocks of our nation. Yet, today, for all of its fundamental importance, the American community is in crisis. Harvard researcher Robert Putnam has documented a massive decline in the levels of social and civic engagement in American communities since 1965. The close-knit neighborhoods of the past have given way to desolate, lifeless suburbs manufactured throughout America in the past four decades. The need to create better communities has never been more urgent.

For me, the effort to create truly outstanding communities—both in the physical and sociological sense is of central personal importance. I consider it my life's work.

The Rev. Culver H. Nelson, Founding Pastor of Church of the Beatitudes

Truth is what you do. It is not an ideological mind set much less a sectarian passion. This is so simply because "acting a belief" is the only final test of its truth.

Power is ephemeral and is only consequential to the current generation. Influence survives and is commonly more important to a future generation than its own. Power dies easily, influence does not. Humans are at their best when they remember the future, that image a dream and shapes it into existence.

When humans look back upon their own lives a certain pattern seems to exist or persist, giving them the feeling that their life was predetermined. No such feeling exists when one seriously regards the future. It is open... freedom for the future is increasingly self-evident. God has created a world to create itself.

Dick Bowers, Scottsdale City Manager

There are no inexorable forces. We are all involved in a "cosmic dance." The unrelenting tug-of-war between ying and yang defines our struggle for balance—no certainty. Consumerism is the most pervasive influence and contradiction in our pursuit of peace and meaning. It drives us, defines us, reduces us and inspires us.

The remarkable beauty and capacity of the human spirit, if nurtured, can be of greater service to society than we imagine. Self-interest too often triumphs over common good.

We must raise the quality and character of public talk as a requisite for healthy sustainable community. It takes courage to do so. Our relationship to each other, to nature, to future generations and to the children among us, needs a vision.

George Land, Chairman & CEO Leadership 2000

After over thirty-five years of research and two decades of consulting with business and governments, I have concluded that our greatest opportunity for the future lies in recovering the open heart and mind that we all knew as children. For centuries our cultures and schools have taught our children a form of thinking that severely limits our capacity to imagine, to choose and to relate. In an era of globalization and of accelerating, turbulent and unpredictable change, these repressed skills and attitudes are those most required to create the family of interdependent humankind.

One powerful example is demonstrated in our studies with children. Below the age of 5, almost 98% of children (across cultures) show an amazingly high capacity to solve problems creatively. By age 10 this has decreased to 30%: by age 15 to 10% and only 2% of adults at age 30 still manifest this high level of creative thinking. We have successfully taught our children judgmental thinking, to follow preconceived notions of what is right and wrong, good and bad, acceptable or unacceptable. So, people end up automatically filtering the information they receive based on past or authoritarian judgments, rather than opening to the authentic reality of the present, they react, repeating old actions rather than asking the new questions, imagining better answers and choosing from a variety of alternatives.

Far more insidious and invidious is the effect this judgmentalism has on our human relationships! We carry forward pre-formed expectations of ourselves and others. True trust, compassion, and love lose out in the constant conflict with what someone once decided "should be." We see the results all around us from violence in the schools, to global religious and ethnic conflicts. These all result from a single source – the pervasive teaching of mental habits of judgmental thinking that separate us from those who are somehow different. More's the pity that we bring all of this home, abandoning authenticity, constantly judging ourselves and then projecting those harsh judgments on others.

We have also learned over the past decade that judgmental thinking can be unlearned. Mountains of research from our own group and others show that organizations, from families to large businesses, can create cultures that foster deep trust, love and active imagination. Creative, authentic, heartfelt leadership is one of the great challenges of our time.

Carl Hodges, Atmospheric Physicist

My current favorite book is *On Dialogue*, by Robert Grudin. Grudin takes a position that most of life can be analyzed in terms of dialogues—usually thought of as with others, but the most important being the continuous one of our life... the dialogue in our head.

Grudin has many good things to say. Two fascinate me daily:

1. "When given a choice between A and B, true freedom is to be able to create C."

2. "We grant ourselves great copiousness, but are restrictive in granting it to others."

I would like to see our exchanges be exercises in granting each other maximum copiousness. I sometimes ponder the fascination with ying and yang metaphors... light recognized by its counterpart of dark, etc. Life to me seems a marvelous continuum.

Max DePree, Chairman Emeritus of Herman Miller, Inc., Member of *Fortune* magazine's National Business Hall of Fame

I believe the behavior of leaders must be understood as a preserving principle of society. A word about what exactly I mean by "leadership." It is not a position. Leadership, to borrow a phrase from John Henry Newman's The Idea of a University, is a "habit of mind." It is not an honor but demanding, hard work. Leadership is not necessarily limited to appointed leaders, but devolves on all kinds of people at all kinds of times, from the people we elect to those who accumulate adulation. All who have followers are leaders.

There will always be dominant and influential leaders with stature and power. The key question in relation to preserving society is whether or not these leaders will hold themselves accountable, but this is insufficient. The examples in our open society are sadly too apparent. You know the examples as well as I do. In the end, only leaders can hold themselves accountable on behalf of the people they serve and lead.

In this sense, then, let me suggest who I believe some of these leaders are:

- Those from whom we learn
- Those who influence the setting of society's agenda
- Those who have visions

- Those who acknowledge the authenticity of persons
- Those who create
- Those who set standards
- Those, like Rosa Parks, who endow us with surprising legacies
- Those who meet the needs of followers
- Those whose behavior and words positively reinforce the best of our society
- Those who trumpet the breaking up and the breaking down of civility
- Those who offer hope and those who say there is no hope
- Those who are the givers, those who are the takers
- Those who scrutinize
- Those who ask the painful and necessary questions
- Those like Mother Teresa who create trust
- Those who understand and actively pursue fairness
- Those who, in our lives, are a safe place
- Those who accept responsibility for their behavior

Leadership is a serious meddling in the lives of other people. Leaders should be able to stand alone, take the heat, bear the pain, tell the truth, and do what's right. Without accountable leaders, no matter how committed or how competent the rest of us are, society will be continually in a state of jeopardy.

David Hankins, Quantum Physicist
aka Jim Carson, Western Artist
- Nature is inexorable, economics and religion are not, but in practice they may be nearly so.
- Religion and economics are more complex matters. Life on earth is controlled overwhelmingly by them.

What is true scientifically?

The Universe exists; we are all subsets of the Universe. The components of our molecules and atoms have been around since the Universe's 'inception,' (or forever if you prefer). As such we know a lot about the Universe through the combination of our conscious mind, our unconscious mind, our corporal make up, and our wave (spiritual) connections with the rest of the Universe. Remember, every particle in the Universe knows every other particle in the Universe. As such, however, we cannot come to know all about the Universe because we are subsets of it. As such, we cannot, in our present form, fully know 'The Mind of God.' Ah, the form, there's the rub! We can, however, significantly know the Universe partially, and that's no mean feat!

Everything except the entire Universe is a lie in that it is not the complete truth. Newton's laws of motion are a lie: Einstein's $E=mc^2$ is a lie, Cezanne's best paintings are a lie, and the outcome of the Forum will be a lie, you can bet on it. So, we must live for the truth in our lies, and that is a significant thing to live for. Goedel said, algebra is a lie, but there is a lot of truth in algebra. I repeat, though, the Universe is absolutely true.

What is true artistically?

Art is a reflection in a medium of our sense of the truth of the Universe. The closer it is to reflecting the Universe, the truer it is and the more beautiful it is. Art and science are the same. Einstein's theories are as great as art, as Mozart's best music is. Anyone who says otherwise is profoundly dumbfounded. The Forum should approach problems it artistically, not pragmatically.

What is true sociologically?

Welfare must be withdrawn to a minimum, but it must be withdrawn very slowly and continuously, not radically. Subsidies that encourage population expansion, especially amongst the poor must be slowly and continuously withdrawn. Poverty should be attacked with incentives toward self improvement and work ethic, not with entitlements. But, at all levels, personal freedom and self expression should be taught and encouraged. This is paramount.

Prejudice is central to our character and must not be squelched as long as behavior is within our legal limits. Prejudice is essential to our free thought, but behavior must be regulated within the law, and it must be regulated without double standard. The enforcement of politically correct dogma, especially with a double standard, is "tyranny over the mind of man." Tyranny is the sociopolitical application of untruth. If man were to always strive to say what is true, tyranny could not exist. Prejudice would exist, but tyranny would perish.

Gloria Feldt, President of Planned Parenthood

At the 1994 United Nations International Conference on Population and Development in Cairo, nearly 180 countries acknowledged that women's health was central to agriculture, environmental erosion, local and global economics, public health and disease management, and of course population stability. Since Cairo, this awareness has only grown more intense, while highlighting some crucial world trends.

There is a definite gender power shift toward greater equilibrium of shared power – economically, in government, and in the home. Women everywhere are challenging traditional, male-dominated cultures and governments in pursuit of social and economic justice and the means to obtain it. These are not just Western aspirations. Just weeks ago, Kuwaiti women cheered each time a member of their nation's parliament voted for allowing women citizens to vote. Although the measure was defeated, the spirit of change is very much alive in Kuwait and throughout the Islamic world.

The credit, I feel, goes to the globalization of ideas and information, particularly family planning and reproductive rights. For American women, better access to family planning meant the ability to make responsible choices. It paved the way for improved literacy, improved economic status, lower fertility rates, and increased involvement in the political process—certainly one of this century's success stories. That success story is going global in the 21st century.

The global gender power shift coincides with Youth-Quake. One billion human beings—a fifth of the world's population, are reaching prime reproductive age. They are the largest generation in history. Another two billion behind them.

Ironically, some have chosen to diminish the importance of population as a global concern, citing falling fertility rates. But if some nations are now on the road to sustainability, it is because they heeded the warning of environmentalists and family planning advocates and took action on issues like family planning, education and economic development.

In the world's poorest nations, continued rapid population growth, fueled by the YouthQuake's population growth momentum, would wipe out gains underway, such as extending school systems, improving health facilities, and providing affordable housing. Women in the developing world stand to be hardest hit.

The direction the global century takes, as well as everyone's quality of life, will be determined in large part by the young women of this generation and the reproductive decisions they make. And by the opportunities they take to include men in those decisions.

Pam Hait, Writer

The December issue of *Fast Company* featured an essay on this problem and poses some intriguing questions:

Fact: We are living in an era of unprecedented value creation and innovation...

Question: If we're making so much progress, how do we account for so much fear of destruction?

Fact: Americans have the highest standard of living on the planet, characterized by convenience and staggering abundance...

Question: If our quality of life is so evolved, why are so many people scrambling to simplify and downshift their lives?

Fact: We're living in an era of dizzying individual freedom, control, and choice...

Question: If things are so good, why do we feel so bad?

Clearly, my children and grandchildren will inherit the cultural and technical advantages of living in the most global of societies. But, if we do not raise the level of dialogue, rediscover our ability to connect and cooperate with each other, and put an end to mindless violence, they will be citizens of a planet where no one feels safe.

My overriding fear is that if we continue in our downward spiral, my children and grandchildren will inherit a world where suspicion replaces trust and violence is the coin of the realm. If this should happen, my grandson and granddaughter will never know the thrill of walking alone down the street to school or riding their bike, on their own, to explore the neighborhood or town.

Sam Campana, Mayor of the City of Scottsdale

Etched over the Schubert Theater in Chicago is the passage, "Only art endures."

And what do we know of pre-history other than the sculpture plucked from shelters in Malta that predate Mesopotamia by 2,000 years or the spirited drawings in a cave in France? Straw soldiers from primitive hogans, mysterious Stonehenge, treasures from pyramids an army of soldiers buried in the fields of rural China. These images tantalize, invoke cultures, illuminate, romance us...

Civilization advanced...warriors immortalized in metal, heroes depicted on murals, every biblical passage painted, royalty memorialized in all art forms. The cemetery itself became a sculpture garden. The Renaissance, graven images, bodies defined (discovered through unauthorized autopsies!), Martha Graham, Shakespeare, impressionism, modernism.

In the past two decades we have reveled in public art, prepared for public consumption, along our public rights-of-way, incorporated into the mundane of required infrastructure, integrated within the here-to-fore invisible wastewater treatment facilities, manhole covers, solid waste sites, electrical substations. Inserting quality of life, thoughtful, whimsical, site-specific fine art into our everyday lives!

This is a new, uniquely American phenomenon. The vanilla of vast roadways might evaporate, murals might mask mediocre walls, and attention might be drawn to the excitement of a major sculpture instead of an empty wasteland.

We are empowering our cultural creators—artists envision the future, dream the untold, paint the unseen, sculpt the imaginary—and you may be offended. It is the history of civilization. The role of public policy. The endurance of art.

Lynne Twist, Advocate and Spokesperson for the End of Hunger, the Preservation of the World's Rainforests and the Emergence of Women

An ancient prophecy about our time: The South American shamans believe that the earth, which they call Pachamama, moves in rhythmic cycles of 500 years. These cycles are called pachakutis. There is a prophecy that says that the tenth pachakuti will be a time of balance and light.

The hallmark of the tenth pachakuti will be the fulfillment of the ancient prophecy of the eagle and the condor. The shamans say that the people of the eagle are those who live in their heads. They are people of the intellect. They are people who, by this time in evolution, will have developed technologies that astound and marvel all humanity. The technological prowess and intellectual potency of the eagles will be at a kind of unprecedented zenith and along with that, will come material wealth beyond imagination. At the same time, the eagles, the people of the modern world, will be spiritually impoverished to their peril.

The people of the condor, refers to the indigenous people, on earth. They are those who live in their hearts and through their five senses. The prophecy says that the condors will be highly evolved in their relationship with the natural world and the world of intuition and wisdom. They will have spiritual wealth beyond their imagination; however, by this time in evolution they will begin to be materially impoverished to their peril.

It is said that the tenth pachakuti is when the eagle

and the condor will rejoin as one and fly together in the same sky, wing to wing. The tenth pachakuti has just begun and the prophecy says that this is the time when the world will come into balance and light.

Richard Daley, Executive Director Arizona-Sonora Desert Museum

Homo sapiens, a late-comer on the evolutionary stage, has been a most remarkable species. Here is a species that compared to many other animals, can't see all that well, can't run all that fast, is not well camouflaged, isn't very strong, can neither breathe underwater nor fly unassisted, and is not very adapted physically for many environments. And yet, this species, our own, has become the dominant species in all of evolutionary time.

This has happened because we have the capacity to learn from experience and to solve complex problems. In short, we are remarkably ingenious.

In the 20th Century, though, our ingenuity has about done us in. We have become the first, living, geophysical force. We have developed technology and habits that can affect global climate, we have caused mass extinctions of other species, and we have depleted our very resource pool. We have even created weapons of mass destruction that can spell the end of our species and many others simultaneously. And, we have been so successful at eliminating the natural controls on our own population size that we have set in motion an increase that may well bring those natural controls back into play in unimaginable ways.

The 21st Century will be the defining moment for Homo sapiens and tens of thousands of our sister species. We will determine whether or not we can restrain ourselves sufficiently to allow for human life and civilization to continue, either at all, or in a way that allows a reasonable semblance of a decent standard of living for many, if not most, people.

Will our ingenuity allow for technological solutions to problems of resource depletion, species extinction, and the myriad associated problems? It may help. In fact, it is the only things that may buy us time to transition to a sustainable world by serving us in four ways:

1. Through technology, we can reduce the per person impact on the environment;
2. We can use technology to raise the standard of living of the poorest among us to a bearable level;
3. It will allow us to study and monitor our impacts more precisely and more quickly than ever;
4. It improves our ability to communicate quickly and to inform the people of the world of the global nature of our problems

But technology is our new alchemy. We want to trust that technology, coupled with a global market economy, will magically solve our problems and that we do not have to face the consequences of massive species extinctions that threaten the ability of the planet to sustain life.

Aristotle noted the relationship between perception and ethics. Today we must change our perception that we are apart from nature to a part of nature and that our lives are inextricably linked to the lives and processes of all the life around us.

The following seven pages include representative articles and quotations that were used to guide and inspire the dialogue as part of the Karakahl Forum

PURPOSE OF THE KARAKAHL FORUM

The words we share today
become the world we will share tomorrow

A human being is part of the whole called by us universe, a part limited in time and space. We experience ourselves, our thoughts, and feelings as something separate from the rest. A kind of optical delusion of consciousness. This delusion is a kind of prison for us, restricting us to our personal desires and to affection for a few persons nearest to us. Our task must be to free ourselves from the prison by widening our circle of compassion to embrace all living creatures and the whole of nature in its beauty... We shall require a substantially new manner of thinking if mankind is to survive.

—Albert Einstein

Such as the words are, such will their affections be esteemed; and such as thrive affections, will be thy deeds; and such as thy deeds will be thy life.

—Socrates

THE KARAKAHL CHALLENGE
To Design Our Preferred Recipe for Reality

PARTIAL LIST OF INGREDIENTS

Optimistic Spirit

Beyond the Facts

Learning From Other Cultures

Open Hearts

Seeing Possibilities

Trust and Commitment

Bridge Building

Wordless Insights

Learning From History

Beyond Formulas

Embracing Mystery

**All with the Intent to be more accurate and
effective in the here and now**

WE CAN'T FORESEE THE FUTURE

Who in the year 1000 could have imagined the course of events over the next millennium? Nothing in that world could have let people foresee the world of today.

Who in 1700 could have predicted the events of the next 100 years—the Enlightenment, Britain's beating France for control of all of North America; the American Revolution, whereby a people created a new nation based on principles inchoate a century before; the French Revolution and the Reign of Terror and the rise of nationalism?

Who in 1800 could have prophesied the world of 1900? This span of time probably saw more fundamental changes than any comparable period—steam replacing horse power, the invention of the telegraph and telephone, skyscrapers, the shrinking of the globe so that one could eat food grown thousands of miles away; mass migrations of people on a scale unmatched since, the expansion of an increasingly democratic America that abolished slavery, and enormous worldwide population growth.

Who in 1900 could have foreseen the hideous ideologies that would kill countless millions of people and nearly destroy civilization? Who 20 years ago, given the bloody history of this era, could have predicted the bloodless collapse of the Soviet Union and the emergence of America as the globe's only superpower, a position of influence never before seen in human history?

Ten years ago (1990), how many people had heard of the Internet? If you had typed the word Internet into a spell checker, the software would have told you that there is no such word. All of this is by way of saying we can't foresee the future except to say that we humans will continue to astonish ourselves by our behavior and misbehavior, our deeds and misdeeds. Let us hope that the advances of recent times will reawaken a sense of awe and well-being, that we will rest easy in the knowledge that there is indeed a God and that we will rediscover and reinvigorate the principles—however imperfectly adhered to—that created this nation: life, liberty and the pursuit of happiness.

—Steve Forbes, Editor-In-Chief

Forbes Magazine

FRAMING THE DIALOGUE

Learn to see in the abstract but not so abstract that you lose your usefulness to society.

—Frank Lloyd Wright

To show that the real is identical with the ideal may roughly be set down as the mainspring of philosophic activity.

—William James

If dialogue is a positive feedback loop in which each participant is incrementally altered by the other's discourse, then surprise is a sudden rush of recognition—sometimes as sharp as the crack of a whip, sometimes as soft as a kiss in a whisper—changing not only all that follows but, by redefinition, all that has gone before. Surprise is, in a sense, the spiritual justification for dialogue and the proof that dialogue is free.

—Robert Grudin

ON NATURE, ART AND ARCHITECTURE

A rock pile ceases to be a rock pile the moment a single man contemplates it, bearing within him the image of a cathedral.

—Antoine de Saint-Exupéry

I know several excellent architects who usually speak feeling and reverentially about nature; how we must harmonize and blend with nature and never violate it. To hear them talk you would think that if they built a house on the side of a hill they would so blend it with nature that you could not see the house until you bumped against it. Actually, they do no such thing. As genuine creators they know that harmony with nature must be achieved on human terms; that, when they bring man and nature together man is the host and nature his guest. The primacy of man must be patent. When a gifted architect finishes his task, a gate built between two ancient trees will look as if the gate were there first and the trees planted afterward. If he builds a house over a creek, the beholder ought not to have the least doubt that the house was there first and the creek brought in later. You do not violate or demean nature by making her your guest. From the beginning of time trees, grass, flowers, birds and animals have felt wholly at home in human habitations, even the city, whereas nature has always been a stern and grudging host.

—Eric Hoffer

The most beautiful thing we can experience is the mysterious. It is the source of all true art and science... Imagination is more important than knowledge. Knowledge is limited. Imagination encircles the world.

—Albert Einstein

ON SCIENCE AND RELIGION

Recently, some physicists have come to see a relationship between their work and the ideas behind Eastern mysticism. They believe that the paradoxes, odds, and probabilities as well as the observer - dependence of quantum mechanics have been anticipated in the writings of Hinduism, Buddhism and Taoism.

—**John Boslough**
Stephen Hawking's Universe

The universe of Eastern mysticism is an illusion. A physicist who attempts to link it with his own work has abandoned physics.

—**Stephen Hawking**

ON OPTIMISM AND PESSIMISM

We stand on a mountain pass in the midst of whirling snow and blinding mist, through which we get glimpses now and then of paths which may be deceptive. If we stand still we shall be frozen to death. If we take the wrong road we shall be dashed to pieces. We do not certainly know whether there is any right one. What must we do? 'Be strong and of good courage.' Act for the best, hope for the best, and take what comes... If death ends all, we cannot meet death better.

—Fitz James Stephens

Please remember that optimism and pessimism are definitions of the world, and that our own reactions on the world, small as they are in bulk, are integral parts of the whole things, and necessarily help to determine the definition. They may even be the decisive elements in determining the definition.

The physicist does not say, "The water will boil anyhow;" he only says it will boil if a fire be kindled beneath it. And so the utmost the student of sociology can ever predict is that if a genius of a certain sort show the way, society will be sure to follow.

—William James

PRODUCTIONDWELLINGS

AN OPPORTUNITY FOR EXCELLENCE

Production Dwellings: An Opportunity for Excellence provides an example of extending design services into areas not generally addressed by the architectural profession. In the late 1960's I directed a seminar on housing and large scale land use planning which received a lot of media coverage. This lead to a request in 1970, from the Wisconsin Department of Natural Resources to research and write about how to improve the appearance and performance of mobile homes. *Production Dwellings* quickly became a nationwide crusade for improving the design of manufactured housing. The publication included a variety of design possibilities, along with inspiring quotations selected from Frank Lloyd Wright's writings. Representative drawings and text are included on the following 11 pages. The significance of the opportunity was the ability to have architecture reach into high-volume production areas where most development actually occurs.

Frank Lloyd Wright quotations that appeared in *Production Dwellings: An Opportunity for Excellence:*

- Vital new forms are needed for environment, new expressions of life as now changed and as it will change continually.

- I do not believe any architecture in the time of commercialism, of industrialism, and of huge organization can be an architecture true to the spirit of those times unless it includes the use of all of these great tools of modern life.

- Standardization should be put to work but never in such a way that it commands the process which yields the original form.

- As for the future, the work shall grow more truly simple; expressive with fewer forms; more articulate with less labor; more plastic; more fluent, although more coherent; more organic. It shall grow...to fit more perfectly the methods and processes that are called upon to produce it.

The Washington Post REAL ESTATE

SATURDAY, JANUARY 15, 1972

Modular Architectural Design Comes to Herndon

By Abbott Combes
Washington Post Staff Writer

Frank Lloyd Wright's architecture is coming to Herndon, Va., more than a decade after the celebrated architect's death.

In what was billed as "a marriage of industry and art," the Frank Lloyd Wright Foundation and the National Homes Corporation revealed a joint venture Thursday to produce industrialized housing units designed by disciples of the influential Mr. Wright.

National Homes also disclosed that it plans a 1,500-unit development of single-family homes, townhouses and garden apartments—all Wright Foundation designs —on property it owns in Herndon near Dulles Airport. David R. Price, executive vice president of the Indiana-based firm, said construction should begin "before the year ends."

In Herndon, town officials indicated they were anxious for the development to begin.

According to Blaise Barnes, the community's land-use analyst, National Homes received approval more than a year ago for a

Duplex townhouse designed by the Frank Lloyd Wright Foundation.

located about one-quarter of a mile northeast of the Dulles access road.

Barnes said that the corporation must still submit

developments and other modular dwellings. Prices for a mobile home to more lot, will range from $4,000 foa mobile home to more

than 400,000 houses and mobile homes since it started 31 years ago. It has annual sales of more than $200 million and also owns a major

Architect Vernon D. Swaback of the Frank Lloyd Wright Foundation, sitting in the living room of the new mobile home, wants this to be a house people will be proud to live in. The different mobile home design will be on the market soon, a real dream come true.

INDOW AND WALL UNITS
DURING SHIPMENT

FOLD-OUT SECTIONS
IN FINAL POSITION

Fold-out window and wall units are used to create a more spacious interior with gently sloping walls. During shipment the sloping portions nest in the storage position, within a twelve foot wide envelope.

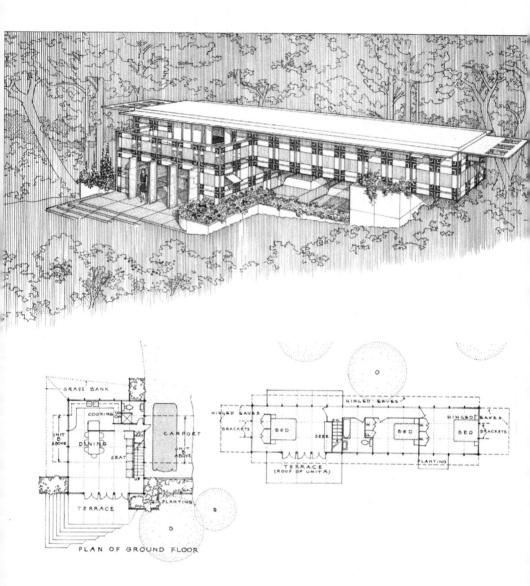

PLAN OF GROUND FLOOR

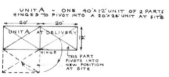

UNIT A — ONE 40'X12' UNIT OF 2 PARTS
HINGED TO PIVOT INTO A 20'X24' UNIT AT SITE

Stacked units and folding eaves allow this modular unit to be shipped fully fabricated. The structural requirements for over-the-road shipment are used in the final setting to provide a carport under the bedroom wing.

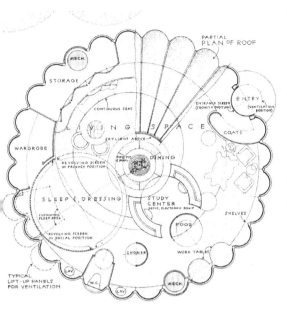

SPACE VALVING:
A house with no conventional partitions or doors. Rooms appear and disappear by way of revolving semi-cylindrical screens. The entire area is one open space which is instantly partitioned at the will of the occupants. The same idea is used for expanded schemes of two or more bedrooms.

ONE ROOM HOUSE:
Total separation of all partitions and cabinetwork from the building allow for the wall-screens, utilities and furnishings to be factory finished and moved in with no cutting or fitting.

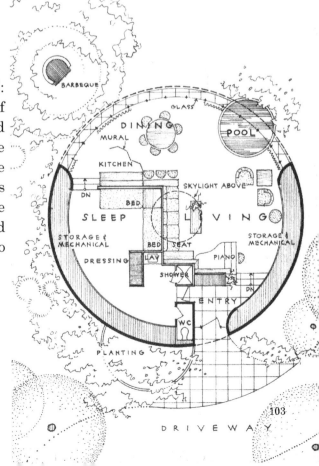

LAND ECONOMICS

a quarterly journal devoted to the study of economic and social institutions

NOVEMBER
1971

VOLUME XLVII
NUMBER 4

Production Dwellings: An Opportunity for Excellence

By VERNON D. SWABACK

In an effort to "make mobile and other factory-built homes fit better into the environment and to encourage manufacturers and developers to work toward improved design and site selection" the State of Wisconsin Department of Natural Resources has made available to the public the findings of a research study which that agency sponsored during 1970. In an explanatory statement the Director of the Bureau of Commercial Recreation of the state agency, Ralph Hovind, wrote: "The mobile home is an increasingly important part of our vacationland scene. Unless greater care is used in placing these factory-built structures in their respective sites, they often tend to clash violently with the natural setting; so much so that many local governments have restricted or discouraged mobile home developments. The booming demand to house the new crop of young marrieds, together with the surge for more vacation homes, comes at a time of tight, costly money. Conventional housing is beyond the grasp of much of the market so many more industrially produced homes (with built-in financing) will be seen. Because of their acknowledged expertise in fitting structures into the landscape, the Taliesin Associated Architects of the Frank Lloyd Wright Foundation were asked to undertake this study. All portions of this work are dedicated to the public by arrangement between the Wisconsin Department of Natural Resources and the Frank Lloyd Wright Foundation." (Editor)

THE COMPOSITE of news articles on the facing page represents a sampling of the coverage attracted by *Production Dwellings*, including a front page story in the *Wall Street Journal*, and coast-to-coast television interviews.

PRODUCTIONDWELLINGS
AN OPPORTUNITY FOR EXCELLENCE

By Rob Cuscaden
Sun-Times Architecture Critic

'Thoughtful simplicity' for mobile homes?

By the Associated Press

Scottsdale, Ariz.

The nation's growing mobile-home industry is producing "older boxes" that "imitate" the newer and crasser urban blight, the Frank Lloyd Wright Foundation charges.

Mobile Homes Design Changes Termed Vital

Taliesin architect says housing industry deplorably polarized

---

ED OLD-FASHIONED BOXES

port Raps Mobile Homes

CARPENTER

Production homes target of Taliesin research

MOST PRESENT MOBILE HOMES, above, have a disorganized facade, their wheels unless covered with aprons, have a box-like shape, are painted white or silver and are packed in long rows so that mobile parks resemble parking

lots. The alternatives in the Taliesin Architects proposal include settled design, planters, earth berms, earth tone colors and imaginative layouts and landscaping.

SECOND PLAN for house manufactured in changeable units by mobile home builder

Assembly-Line Houses

"It is amazing to find how low-cost housing in America is the crying need of the hour. I feel that it is the most important field that we have and it has been neglected by our architects."

Frank Lloyd Wright, the late-great architect,

FOURTH HOUSE, like soup dish upside down, has revolving inner walls

TALIESIN

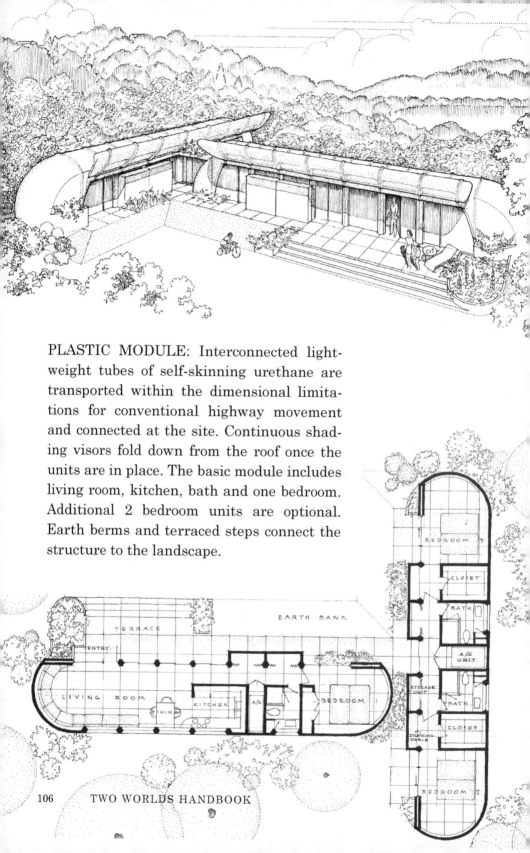

PLASTIC MODULE: Interconnected lightweight tubes of self-skinning urethane are transported within the dimensional limitations for conventional highway movement and connected at the site. Continuous shading visors fold down from the roof once the units are in place. The basic module includes living room, kitchen, bath and one bedroom. Additional 2 bedroom units are optional. Earth berms and terraced steps connect the structure to the landscape.

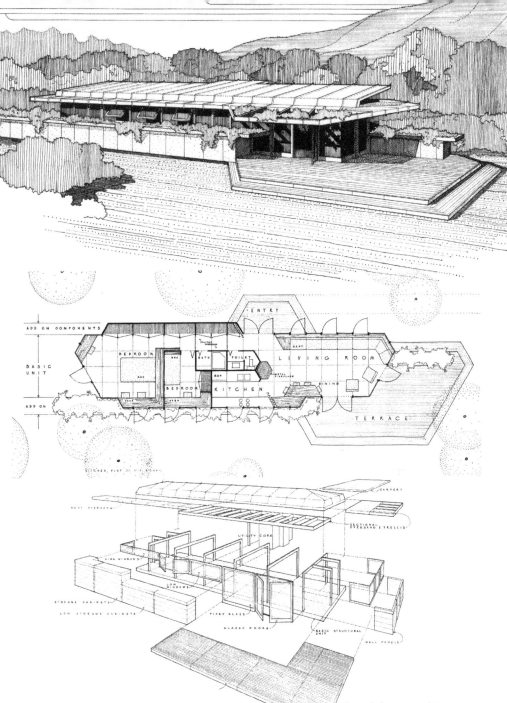

THE UNIT HOUSE: A modular design with add-on units stored inside the module during delivery. An expansive platform terrace and planting boxes help to integrate the house with its setting.

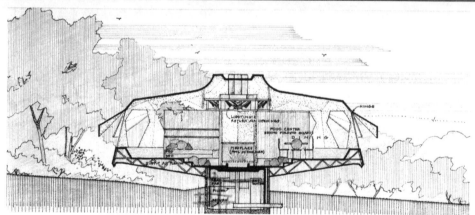

The prefabricated Petalform House is shipped in densely stacked components for assembly on-site in a variety of configurations from a one room house to the Family Tryptych shown on the facing page. Automated "petals" open and close, following the path of the sun over alternating glazed and screened openings.

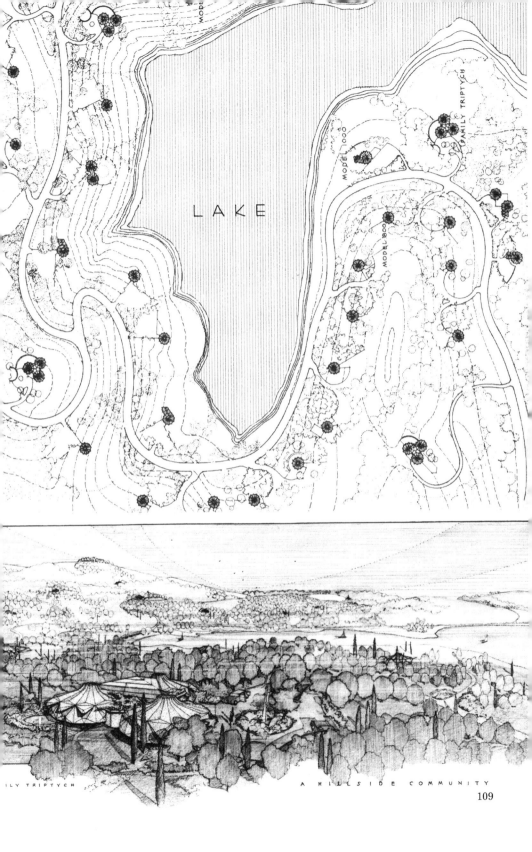

LAKE

MODEL 1000

MODEL 1200

MODEL 1800

FAMILY TRIPTYCH

ILY TRIPTYCH

A HILLSIDE COMMUNITY

THE GOVERNING BOARD

The initial Board has been limited to three individuals in order that the Foundation's mission may be communicated more globally before considering the addition of other directors.

VERNON D. SWABACK

A native of Chicago, Vernon D. Swaback began his architectural training at the University of Illinois. In 1957 he became Frank Lloyd Wright's youngest apprentice, spending summers at Taliesin in Wisconsin and winters at Taliesin West in Arizona. In 1978 he left the Wright organization to found Vernon Swaback Associates, a firm of architects and planners.

In 1999 he and his long-term associates, John E. Sather and Jon C. Bernhard founded Swaback Partners. Together they have received more than 80 local, regional and national honors and awards in widely varying areas of their involvements, including the design of water conserving environments, pioneering in sustainable design, community visioning, public art, the design of all residential and building types and the planning and urban design of communities for both the private and public sectors.

Swaback served as chairman of the Frank Lloyd Wright Foundation and on the boards of various think tank organizations and is now on the Executive Board of StarShine Academy, a K-12 Charter School, and President of Cattletrack Arts and Preservation, a foundation dedicated to supporting the arts and historic preservation. He is a registered architect in 15 states from California to Connecticut and has the distinction of having been inducted into the College of Fellows by both the American Institute of Architects and the American Institute of Certified Planners. His books include, *Designing the Future* (1997), *The Custom Home* (2001), *The Creative Community* (2003), *Designing with Nature* (2005), *Creating Value, Smart Development and Green Design* (2007), *Believing in Beauty* (2009) and *Living in Two Worlds: The Creative Path to Community* (2010).

TOM MARTINSON

Tom Martinson is a city-planning consultant and architectural historian, with an international practice based in Minneapolis. He has worked as a designer for several architectural firms; as an architectural historian for the National Park Service Historic American Buildings Survey and the U.S. Commission of Fine Arts; and in the 1970s was Principal Planner for the City of Minneapolis with lead design responsibility for neighborhood revitalization and downtown economic development. He has carried out architectural field studies of hundreds of cities and sites, on all inhabited continents.

In private practice since 1985, Martinson has worked in development planning throughout the United States and in several Asia-Pacific countries. Project settings ranged in scales from a Mojave Desert mining town in California to densely populated cities like Seoul. He was principal consultant for the 1987 Downtown St. Louis Plan. In the mid-1900s he served as planning manager for the US$15 billion Bonifacio Global City in Manila, and was project planner for the master plan of an 800-acre, ecologically based seaside resort in southern Luzon. He was regional planning consultant during master planning of the new University of Technology Petronas in Malaysia.

Martinson has applied his continuing practice experience to lectures, articles, and books on architecture and urbanism. His publications include *A Guide to the Architecture of Minnesota*, with David Gebhard; *American Dreamscape: The Pursuit of Happiness in Postwar Suburbia*; and *The Atlas of American Architecture: 2000 Years of Architecture, City Planning, Landscape Architecture, and Civil Engineering*.

LAURA TEMPLETON

To lay the groundwork for the Foundation's global outreach, we are pleased to have the expertise of board member Laura Templeton. For the past 11 years, she served as Vice President for Business Development at the Urban Land Institute in Washington, DC during which the organization's revenues increased tenfold. She directed all national and international new business development, advertising, multi-media, trade shows, sponsorship sales and corporate marketing for North America, Europe and Asia; she was responsible for managing client, underwriter, stakeholder, and investor relations, as well as managing media relations with *The Wall Street Journal* and related industry media.

She has sourced new business markets; developed

and fostered effective, lucrative long-term working relationships with clients, constituents, and corporate affiliates in 50 countries.

Templeton received a Bachelors of Arts, Magna Cum Laude in Marketing and Merchandising from Barry University in Miami, Florida. Her first six years in business included managing corporate advertising and marketing for Allied and Federated Retail stores in Miami, Los Angeles and Dallas. The next nine years were spent developing and executing corporate sales and marketing real estate relationships with major developers, including Trammell Crow Companies and Mel Simon Properties.

From 1991 to 1999 she was Public Relations Director for the Dallas Cowboys Football Franchise and marketing and sales manager for a variety of national enterprises including publications, trade shows, corporate branding, advertising and sales campaigns. She is the Corporate Director of Commercial Development Programs for Leo A. Daly Architecture, Planning, Engineering and Interiors, a major multi-disciplinary design-based firm with an international practice.

Designing
The
Future

Designing
with
Nature

Vernon D. Swaback, FAIA, FAICP

THE CREATIV
COMMUNI
Designing for Life

Vernon D. Swaback, FAIA, FA

THE ATLAS OF AMERICA
ARCHITECTURE

CREATING VALUE

Smart Development
and Green Design

Vernon D. Swaback FAIA, FAICP

Urban Land
Institute

TOM MARTINSON

**2000 Years of Architecture, City Planning,
Landscape Architecture, and Civil Engineering**

Believing
in Beauty

Conversations with Vernon D. Swaback

AMERICAN DREAMSCAPE
THE PURSUIT OF HAPPINESS IN POSTWAR SUBURBIA
TOM MARTINSON

Our Heritage: *This compos
of books by Vernon D. Swaba
and Tom Martinson refle
an understanding of what
worked best in the past and
vision for what will work e
better in the future.*

Excerpts from the
TWO WORLDS COMMUNITY
FOUNDATION 1023 FILING
with the Internal Revenue Service

We must love our children enough to design a

world which instructs them toward community,

ecology, responsibility and joy.

— **David W. Orr**

Two Worlds Community Foundation (the "Foundation") was established in December 2009 to research, communicate, and cultivate the ecological, technological, behavioral, and economic relationships required for the sustainable design and development of humanity's built environments.

The term Two Worlds Community refers to the Two Worlds in which we live:

The "Operational World" in which we carry out our daily affairs, involving economic markets and financial transactions, political forums, sporting events, entertainment and fashion—a world of "me" in which commitments and transactions tend to favor short-term thinking; and the "Sustaining World" consisting of the natural ecosystems from which we derive the basic necessities of life as well as the more holistic and "spiritual" dimensions of human existence representative in education, science, religion, arts and culture—a world of "we" in which nature, spirit, behavior, and commitments tend to be long-term.

The Foundation was formed to help cultivate our Two Worlds into a single sustainable community. By initiating and supporting focused exploration, analysis, and modeling of sustainable practices in the design and construction of our built space, the Foundation will address the multiple issues of human habitation in a more integrated way than what has historically resulted from the combination of standardized codes and ordinances and the daily transactions in the private and public sectors. The Foundation's activities will be aimed at promoting and advancing the design of physical environments that encourage and inspire positive relationships between individuals and between all of humanity and nature.

FOUNDERS AND PROFESSIONAL TEAM

The initial founding force behind the Foundation is Vernon D. Swaback, prominent architect and planner. Swaback has written and lectured extensively on matters relating to architecture, design and development, and has a long history of involvement with charitable organizations.

From the time of his living at Taliesin West while studying and working with Frank Lloyd Wright, Swaback has had a vision and passion for cultivating safe and sustainable communities. This commitment, together with Swaback's distinguished career as an architect and planner and his involvement with nonprofit organizations, has culminated in an acute awareness that the design and construction of truly sustainable communities is vital to the very survival of the human race, yet cannot be achieved solely by the efforts of market transactions or government interventions.

To help shape the Foundation's mission and begin implementing its activities, Swaback enlisted two additional directors, Tom Martinson and Laura Templeton, both of whom bring a wealth of experience and insight.

Martinson is a city-planning consultant and architectural historian, with an international practice based in Minneapolis. He has worked as a designer for several architectural firms; as an architectural historian for the National Park Service Historic American Buildings Survey and the U.S. Commission of Fine Arts; and in the 1970s was Principal Planner for the City of Minneapolis with lead design responsibility for neighborhood revitalization and downtown economic development. He has applied his continuing practice experience to lectures, articles, and books on architecture and urbanism.

Laura Templeton currently serves as the Corporate Business Development/Relationship Director for Leo A. Daly Architecture, Planning, Engineering and Interiors, a major multi-disciplinary design-based firm with an international practice. Prior to joining Leo A. Daly, Templeton worked for many years at the Urban Land Institute in Washington, D.C., where she served as Vice President for Business Development, helping the organization's revenues increase tenfold, and directed all national and international new business development, advertising, multi-media, trade show, sponsorship sales and corporate marketing for North America, Europe and Asia.

As the Foundation grows and begins implementing its programs, it is anticipated that the initial directors will identify other qualified individuals with a demonstrated commitment to advancing sustainable practices in our built environment, to also serve on the board of directors.

THE NEED FOR THE FOUNDATION:
From the World of Design to the Design of the World

Never before in human history has our collective impact on nature's ecosystem services been so threatening. Humanity's geometrically expanding impact on the workings of nature, now threatens the future of our existence.

There is an urgent need for more informed human behavior and long-range commitments beyond the short-term interests of the marketplace, with its tendency to commodify every facet of human life, even when the marketplace is subsidized by well-meaning public sector support. No long-term success is possible without enlightened and significant accomplishments in the here and now.

The Foundation was formed to address the multiple issues of human habitation in a far more integrated way than what typically results from the combination of standardized codes, ordinances, market transactions, and government interventions.

THE FOUNDATION'S VISION
A Sustainable Two Worlds Community

The Two Worlds Community refers to the dualities that constitute our lifetime experience.

The more evident "Operational World" dominates daily news and is central to fluctuations in both local and global markets. Its activities and focus tend to be linear, political, and popular. These tendencies play out in our easily shared interests in sports, fashion, celebrity, food, wine and dieting, all of which constitute our most familiar conversational "reality."

The less evident "Sustaining World" includes the ecosystem services of nature and the more holistic and "spiritual" aspects of human endeavors represented in education, science, religion, technology, arts and culture. This world involves a more integrated long-term sense of what it means to be human, taking into account the full range of human experience, from the basic necessities of food and shelter to the most advanced forms of high art and culture.

The Foundation's vision contemplates the future as a time of unprecedented demand for creativity and service. The Two Worlds Community premise is that there will be a holistically designed future for humanity, or there will be no human future. The Foundation exists to bring together the Operational and Sustaining Worlds into a cohesive community where both interests complement and profit from the other under the direction of a coherent system of accounting.

THE FOUNDATION'S MISSION
Research, Communicate, and Cultivate a Sustainable "Two Worlds" Community

Design shapes both our personal and shared experiences. Design is the fundamental integration between the nature we inherit, the technology we invent, and the behaviors we practice. Design is the rudder of culture, marshalling the use of the earth's resources, creating beauty in the physical environment, and helping to shape the meaning of life itself.

The Foundation's mission is to research, showcase, and cultivate harmonious "Two Worlds" communities; to address the multiple issues of human habitation in a far more integrated way than what typically results from the combination of standardized codes, ordinances, and market transactions; and to promote and advance the design of physical environments that are holistic in ways that lie beyond what market transactions or government interventions have historically produced or suggest to be the limits of what is possible.

THE FOUNDATION'S ACTIVITIES
Research, Communicate, Cultivate

Overview of the Foundation's programs will include:

- Conducting and sponsoring research,
- Publishing newsletters and books consistent with the Foundation's exempt purposes,
- Conducting global design competitions,
- Organizing seminars and forums for advanced discussions on sustainable development, and
- Designing and implementing (or helping to implement) pilot projects, consistent with the Foundation's mission and its tax-exempt status, that model the Foundation's vision, addressing the urgent need for a more informed and long-range approach to the shaping of our built environment.

These initiatives will leverage the resources of governments, academic institutions, private enterprise, and nongovernmental organizations to explore, develop, and implement holistic Two Worlds Community proposals and best practices.

Initially, it is anticipated that the Foundation will focus approximately 50 to 70 percent of its resources on research, publications, and design competitions; 20 to 30 percent on seminars; and 10 to 20 percent on cultivating community development projects. The activities of the Foundation will be governed by its Board of Directors, and will be carried out by volunteers and, eventually, paid executive staff.

Detail regarding each category of planned activities, including an explanation of how each proposed activity furthers the Foundation's exempt purposes, are provided below.

The Foundation will conduct and sponsor research directly relating to its charitable, educational, and scientific purposes, and will add its research and insights to that of others, all in search of greater clarity for how to better design the settlements of earth.

Research will include topics such as sustainable design, ecologically-integrated architecture, environmentally-compatible design technologies, renewable energy, shared resource initiatives, sustainable landscape practices, the role of design and community planning in preserving and promoting indigenous cultures and indigenous wildlife. The Foundation will carry out this research through formal and informal surveys and questionnaires submitted to community organizations, government agencies, educational organizations, and private enterprises; interviews with informed individuals and groups; secondary research of relevant published material in academic publications, industry and trade journals, government reports, white papers, and other such sources; and other generally accepted forms of primary and secondary research. It is anticipated that research projects will be selected by the directors as they establish and implement the Foundation's vision and mission.

All research will be conducted in a manner that serves the public interest (the betterment of humanity as a whole), and not private interests. Research results will be made available to the public on a nondiscriminatory basis, either at no charge or for a nominal fee intended to cover a portion of the costs of publication. Research results will be made available to the interested public in the form of books, articles, newsletters, white papers, and online media.

At this time, it is not anticipated that the Foundation will perform research on behalf of or at the request of third parties, other than possibly for the benefit of other 501(c)(3) organizations or community groups, to the extent that such research serves a broad public purpose consistent with the Foundation's exempt purposes. The Foundation does not anticipate undertaking any research pursuant to contracts with private industries, including Swaback Partners or other private interests associated with the founders, directors, substantial contributors, or other individuals affiliated with the Foundation.

Research: Systems Integration

A variety of programs will be structured to begin where other studies leave off. For example, preparing educational material that would be accessible to and beneficial for the general public, including simple case studies, illustrations, and statistics—something compellingly clear and useful—showcasing various methods and means of movement, including walking, the use of non-motorized devices (bicycles), segues, personal vehicles, shared vehicles (taxis, zip cars, etc.), vans, buses, light rail, high speed trains, sea and air transport, and finally, virtual and voice contact at the speed of light.

The objective of the Foundation's "systems integration" research will be to rise above preconceived judgments of being "for or against" a particular method or approach, in order to understand individual modes in symphonically related terms. The aim will be to cultivate a vision of our built space that benefits from an orchestrated and nuanced examination of how the constituent elements of design and construction can work together to shape a community that seamlessly integrates the "Operational World" of our daily affairs and transactions and the "Sustaining World" consisting of the natural ecosystems from which we derive the basic necessities of life and the deeper more "spiritual" dimensions of human existence.

Communicate: Publications

The Foundation will fund, write (or cause to be written) and publish newsletters, books, articles, white papers, and online media with a focus on ideas, studies, proposals and living examples of the urgent, joyful, life-enriching, power and integrative value of community.

The over-arching purpose of all such publications will be to instruct, enlighten, and engage the general public on a wide range of subjects, useful to individuals and beneficial to the community as a whole, relating to the Foundation's vision of a sustainable two worlds community. All materials published by the Foundation will contain educational content, will be prepared and presented using methods generally accepted as "educational" in character, will be distributed in a manner that furthers the organization's educational and scientific purposes, and will be published in a manner that is distinguishable from ordinary commercial publishing practices.

The Foundation anticipates that it will offer its publications to the general public at no charge, or at a nominal charge intended to recover a portion of the publication costs. Publications will not be provided to private interests directly or indirectly affiliated with the Foundation (including Swaback Partners) on terms more favorable than those offered to the general public. It is anticipated that the Foundation will hold all intellectual property rights relating to its published material.

Communicate: Seminars

As the Foundation's activities and fund-raising develop, it is anticipated that the Foundation will organize and host conferences, seminars, and public discussions relating to the Foundation's vision and various aspects of its mission. Topics will be selected by the Foundation's directors, executive staff, and/or teams of qualified individuals assembled for the purpose of planning a particular event. All topics will relate to the Foundation mission and will be aimed at furthering its exempt purposes. It is anticipated that event topics will share themes and subject matters with the Foundation's published materials; for example, sustainable design, ecologically-integrated architecture, environmentally-compatible design technologies, shared resource initiatives, and systems integration.

It is anticipated that some of these events (for example, community forums) will be offered free of charge, while others (such as seminars with a more in-depth focus featuring distinguished presenters and panelists) will require a reasonable fee to attend, to offset some of the costs of sponsoring the event. It is also anticipated that the Foundation will make available to the general public recordings of Foundation events - on DVD, audiotape, or electronic media - which will be available free of charge or for a nominal fee intended to cover the costs of producing such materials. The Foundation will retain all intellectual property rights to the materials that it publishes.

Cultivate: Design Competitions

In furtherance of its educational mission, the Foundation will sponsor local to global design competitions, offering awards to the winners and publishing the achievements and/or securing publicity for the winners in appropriate academic or industry journals.

The underlying purpose, emphasis, and methodology of the design competitions will be to showcase innovative yet workable approaches to holistic environmental design. In all cases, the design exploration will be for solutions that go beyond what the for-profit world and traditional government interventions can easily deliver, but not so far as to make the proposals seem irrelevant or impracticable. An example of the intended competition would be a digitized photo and drawing-illustrated presentation of one or more existing communities that are beautiful and sustainable, including a multi-generational record of energy, industry and creativity. Other competitions might center on not-yet existing, but proposed communities of the applicants' own design, suitable for consideration in the here and now, indicating who would be attracted to the ideas and able to create and sustain the designer's proposals for beneficial ways of living.

It is anticipated that these design competitions will be adjudicated by a jury comprised of Foundation directors and staff and qualified outside individuals. Depending on the nature and subject of a particular competition, submissions may be open to community groups; academic institutions and programs; students, professionals, and other individuals; governmental entities; and private enterprises. Requests for submissions will be made in Foundation literature (e.g., newsletters, website, etc.), appropriate academic and industry publications, and other relevant media.

Individuals and entities affiliated with the Foundation (including Swaback Partners and individuals working for Swaback Partners) or with individuals serving on a jury for a particular competitions will be ineligible to participate.

Cultivate: Pilot Community Development Projects

Frank Lloyd Wright was often asked how it felt, "to be so far ahead of his time." He objected to the question, saying, "The time for an idea to happen is as soon as someone has it and the ability to carry it out." Among the most important activities of the Foundation will be to support the design and implementation of pilot building and community endeavors in a variety of types, sizes and locations, consistent with the Foundation's charitable and educational purposes, wherever opportunities for sustainable projects present themselves.

The Foundation's directors and executive staff will carefully look for and consider potential community development projects that further the Foundation's exempt purposes and are consistent with established IRS regulations and guidelines.

As the Foundation builds its funding, it will begin exploring opportunities to develop community projects aimed at providing relief of the poor and distressed; eliminating discrimination and prejudice; and relieving, combating, and preventing community deterioration in ways that have not been achieved through historical government intervention or market-based transactions. The Foundation will seek to accomplish these objectives by designing and constructing communities in a more holistic and integrated way. The focus of such projects will be to develop pilot projects offering a road map to a future of sustainable communities that function as an integrated whole, with vibrantly holistic ecological, technological, behavioral, and economic relationships.

In addition, or as alternative basis for furthering the Foundation's exempt purposes, future community development projects may be aimed at lessening the burdens of government; assisting persons in specific racial groups to acquire housing for the purpose of stabilizing neighborhoods or reducing racial imbalances; lessening neighborhood tensions (by, for example, addressing poverty and community deterioration associated with overcrowding in lower income areas in which ethnic or racial tensions are high); and/or providing for the more specific needs of the elderly or physically disabled.

Cultivate: American Indian Communities

One specific example of the type of community development projects the Foundation intends to pursue is a focused initiative to address the severe need for holistic, culturally appropriate, sustainable housing on American Indian reservations.

There are 561 federally recognized tribes in the United States, including 229 Alaska Native Villages. More than three-quarters of a million Native Americans live on reservations or in other tribal areas (another 1.68 million live outside tribal areas). On many Indian reservations, housing conditions lag far behind those of the general U.S. population, with high rates of homelessness or under-housed populations; high rates of overcrowding; homes in poor physical condition; a lack of plumbing and basic utility services; and very little, if any, mortgage lending.

The National American Indian Housing Council (NAIHC) reports that approximately 200,000 housing units are needed immediately in Indian country, while approximately 90,000 Native families are homeless or under-housed. The Native American homeownership rate is estimated to be as low as 33%, lowest among all ethnic groups and less than half the rate for the general U.S. population (in 2004). See NAIHC, Indian Housing FACT SHEET, attached as Appendix H. Even for tribal members with good income, building a home within their community is extremely difficult due to the absence of mortgage lending on Indian reservations and other legal roadblocks. Attached as Appendix I is a January 7, 2010, Indian Country Today article, discussing the extremely low volume of mortgage loans on Indian reservations, despite a determined effort to end the effective red-lining of Native homelands that began in the second half of the 1990s, and explaining some of the roadblocks that Native Americans face when attempting to secure mortgage financing.

Many of the housing needs on Indian lands are tied directly to economic conditions and forces. The poverty rate for Native Americans is approximately 26%–2.6 times higher than that for whites and more than twice the average for all Americans. The unemployment rate for Indians living in Indian areas has remained more than twice as high as the rest of the United States.

Yet, housing within American Indian reservations is not just an economic issue; it is also deeply intertwined with, and significantly impacts, larger social, cultural, political, environmental, and spiritual dimensions. In many Native American communities, the home is considered a cornerstone of community and traditional culture, and the foundation for all planning. These more subtle "sustainable world" considerations have been largely overlooked in the historical government-provided approach to Indian housing as well more modern transactional-based approaches to providing affordable housing on Indian reservations.

As the Foundation establishes its funding, it will begin exploring opportunities to work with one or more Indian tribes, tribal enterprises, or Native American organizations to develop pilot projects on Indian reservations aimed at fostering sustainable, culturally-based, integrated communities. Such projects will further the

Foundation's charitable, educational, and scientific purposes by eliminating discrimination and prejudice (e.g., the historic red-lining of Indian reservations); relieving, combating, and preventing community deterioration; and providing stability through the thoughtful, integrated design and construction of sustainable model communities in ways that have not been achieved through historic government housing programs on Indian reservations.

The Foundation will explore a variety of options for financing such projects, including tax exempt bond financing, tribal economic development bonds, low-income housing tax credits, funding for tribal housing under the Native American Housing and Self Determination Act (NAHASDA), and other such funds, but the Foundation's efforts will focus on opportunities to go beyond what has resulted from historical government housing programs or more recent attempts at market-based affordable housing initiatives.

The focus of the Foundation's American Indian Housing Initiative will be to work alongside Indian tribal leaders and communities (as opposed to an outside-in or top-down approach), to develop pilot projects that offer a road map to a future of sustainable communities on Indian reservations that function as an integrated whole, with vibrantly holistic ecological, technological, behavioral and economic relationships. As such, these pilot projects will further the Foundation's educational purposes, by providing new approaches to building (or rebuilding) communities that may be replicated in other contexts. It is anticipated that these projects will also have the benefit of lessening the burdens of the federal and tribal governments, which historically have had a nearly exclusive responsibility for housing on Indian reservations.

REFERENCES

Balish, Chris. *How to Live Well Without Owning a Car.* Berkeley: Ten Speed Press, 2006.

Bellah, Robert N., Richard Madsen, William M. Sullivan, Ann Swidler, and Steven M. Tipton. *Habits of the Heart, Individualism and Commitment in American Life.* New York: Harper & Row, 1985.

Block, Peter. *The Answer to How is Yes: Acting on What Matters.* San Francisco: Berrett-Koehler Publishers, Inc., 2002

Brockman, John (Editor). *What Are You So Optimistic About?.* New York: Harper Perennial, 2007.

Brown, Lester R. *Plan B 4.0: Mobilizing to Save Civilization.* New York: W.W. Norton & Company, 2009.

Bruegmann, Robert. Sprawl: *A Compact History.* Chicago: The University of Chicago Press, 2005.

Burleigh, Michael. *Sacred Causes: The Clash of Religion and Politics, From the Great War to the War on Terror.* New York: HarperCollins, 2007.

Crawford, J.H. Carfree Cities. *The Netherlands*: International Books, 1977.

Csikszentmihalyi, Mihaly. *Flow: The Psychology of Optimal Experience.* New York: Harper Perenial, 1990.

De Bono, Edward. *I am Right You Are Wrong: From Rock Logic to Water Logic.* New York: Viking, 1990, 1991.

Deloria, Vine. *God is Red: A Native View of Religion.* Golden: Fulcrum Publishing, 2003.

Ehrenhalt, Alan. *The Lost City: Discovering the Forgotten Virtues of Community in the Chicago of the 1950's.* New York: BasicBooks, 1995.

Einstein, Albert. *The World as I See It.* New York: Citadel Press, 1956.

Etzioni, Amitai. T*he Spirit of Community: The Reinvention of American Society.* New York: Touchstone, 1993.

Farson, Richard. *The Power of Design: A Force for Transforming Everything.* Norcross, Georgia: Greenway Communications, 2008.

Finkelstein, Israel and Neil Silberman. *The Bible Unearthed: Archaeology's New Vision of Ancient Israel and the Origin of its Sacred Texts.* New York: Simon and Schuster, 2002.

Fox, Mathew. *Original Blessing.* Santa Fe, New Mexico: Bear & Company, 1983.

Freed, Judah. *Global Sense: Awakening Your Personal Power for Democracy and World Peace.* Colorado: Media Visions Press, 2006.

Gardner, James. *The Intelligent Universe: AI, ET and the Emerging Mind of the Cosmos*. Franklin Lakes, NJ: New Page Books, 2007.

Gardner, John. *Self-Renewal: The Individual and the Innovative Society*. New York: W.W. Norton & Company, 1981.

Geering, Lloyd. *Christianity Without God*. Polebridge Press, 2002.

Girardet, Herbert. Cities *People Planet: Liveable Cities for a Sustainable World*. Chichester: John Wiley & Sons Ltd., 2004.

Girardet, Herbert and Mendonca, Miguel. *A Renewable World: Energy, Ecology, Equality – A Report for the World Future Council*. London: Green Books, 2009.

Greene, Brian. *The Elegant Universe, Superstrings, Hidden Dimensions, and the Quest for the Ultimate Theory*. New York: W.W. Norton & Company, 1999.

Handy, Charles. *Beyond Certainty: The Changing Worlds of Organizations*. Boston: Harvard Business School Press, 1996.

Handy, Charles. *The Hungry Spirit: Beyond Capitalism, A Quest for Purpose in the Modern World*. New York: Broadway Books, 1998.

Hansen, James. *Storms of My Grandchildren: The Truth About the Coming Climate Catastrophe and Our Last Chance to Save Humanity.* New York: Bloomsbury, 2009.

Hartmann, Thom. *The Last Hours of Ancient Sunlight: The Fate of the World and What We Can Do Before It's Too Late.* New York: Three Rivers Press, 2004.

Hartmann, Thom. *The Prophet's Way: A Guide to Living in the Now.* Rochester, Vermont: Park Street Press, 1997 & 2004.

Hawken, Paul. *Blessed Unrest: How the Largest Movement in the World Came into Being and Why No One Saw It Coming.* New York: Penguin Group, 2007.

Hawken, Paul, Amory Lovins and L. Hunter Lovins. *Natural Capitalism, Creating the Next Industrial Revolution.* Boston: Little, Brown and Company, 1999.

Hock, Dee. *Birth of the Chaordic Age.* San Francisco: Berrett-Koehler Publishers, Inc., 1999.

Jones, Robert. God, Galileo and Geering: *A Faith for the 21st Century.* Santa Rosa, California: Polebridge Press, 2005.

Keller, Suzanne. *Community: Pursuing the Dream, Living the Reality.* Princeton and Oxford: Princeton University Press, 2003.

Klaus, Susan L. *A Modern Arcadia: Frederick Law Olmsted Jr. and the Plan for Forest Hills Gardens.* Amberst & Boston: University of Massachusetts Press, 2002.

Kotkin, Joel. *The New Geography: How the Digital Revolution is Reshaping the American Landscape.* New York: Random House, 2000.

Kotkin, Joel. *The Next 100 Million: America in 2050.* New York: The Penguin Press, 2010.

Leopold, Aldo. *A Sand County Almanac.* London: Oxford University Press, 1949.

Lewis, Michael. *The Big Short: Inside the Doomsday Machine.* New York: W.W. Norton, 2010.

Martinson, Tom. *American Dreamscape: The Pursuit of Happiness in Postwar Suburbia.* New York: Carroll & Graf Publishers, 2000.

Martinson, Tom. *The Atlas of American Architecture: 2000 Years of Architecture, City Planning, Landscape Architecture, and Civil Engineering.* New York: Rizzoli International Publications, Inc., 2009.

Mau, Bruce, Jennifer Leonard, and The Institute Without Boundaries. *Massive Change.* New York: Phaidon, 2004.

McKibben, Bill. *Deep Economy: The Wealth of Communities and the Durable Future.* New York: Times Books, Henry Holt and Company, 2007.

McKibben, Bill. *Hope, Human and Wild: True Stories of Living Lightly on the Earth*. Boston: Little, Brown and Company, 1995.

Meade, Michael. *The World Behind the World: Living at the Ends of Time*. Seattle: Greenfire Press, 2008.

Needleman, Jacob. *Money and the Meaning of Life*. New York: Currency Doubleday, 1984.

Nisbett, Richard E. *The Geography of Thought: How Asian's and Westerners Think Differently... and Why*. New York: Free Press, 2003.

Orr, David W. *Ecological Literacy: Education and the Transition to a Postmodern World*. Albany: State University of New York Press, 1992.

Orr, David W. *The Nature of Design: Ecology, Culture, and Human Intention*. New York: Oxford University Press, 2002.

Osbon, Diane K. (Editor). *Reflections on the Art of Living: A Joseph Campbell Companion*. New York: HarperCollins, 1991.

Osler, Sir William. *A Way of Life*. New York: Dover Publications, 1951.

Robbins, John. *Healthy at 100: How You Can - at Any Age – Dramatically Increase Your Life Span and Your Health Span*. New York: Ballantine Books, 2006.

Rybczynski, Witold. *City Life: Urban Expectations in a New World*. New York: Scribner, 1995.

Sachs, Jeffrey D. *The Edge of Poverty: Economic Possibilities for Our Time*. New York: The Penguin Press, 2005.

Sieden, Lloyd Steven. *Buckminster Fuller's Universe: His Life and Work*. Cambridge, Massachusetts: Perseus Publishing, 1989.

Speth, James G. *Red Sky at Morning: American and the Crisis of the Global Environment*. New Haven and London: Yale University Press, 2004.

Speth, James G. *The Bridge at the Edge of the World: Capitalism, the Environment and Crossing from Crisis to Sustainability*. New Haven: Yale University Press, 2008.

Spong, John Shelby. *A New Christianity for a New World: Why Traditional Faith is Dying and How a New Faith is Being Born*. San Francisco: HarperCollins, 2001.

Sucher, David. *City Comforts: How to Build an Urban Village*. Seattle: City Comforts, Inc., 2003.

Swaback, Vernon D. *Believing in Beauty*. Phoenix: Bridgewood Press, 2009.

Swaback, Vernon D. *Smart Growth: Smart Development and Green Design*. Washington, D.C.: Urban Land Institute, 2007.

Thackara, John. *In the Bubble, Designing in a Complex World*. Cambridge, Massachusetts and London: The MIT Press, 2006.

Todd, Nancy Jack, and John. *From Eco-Cities to Living Machines, Principles of Ecological Design*. Berkeley, California: North Atlantic Books, 1993.

Turner, Frederick. *The Culture of Hope, A New Birth of the Classical Spirit*. New York: The Free Press, 1995.

Unwin, Raymond. *Town Planning in Practice: An Introduction to the Art of Designing Cities and Suburbs*. Princeton and Oxford: Princeton University Press, 1994.

Wilson, Edward O. *The Creation: An Appeal to Save Life on Earth*. New York: W.W. Norton & Company, 2006.

Wilson, Edward O. *The Future of Life*. New York: Alfred A. Knopf, 2002.

Wright, Frank Lloyd. *The Living City*. New York: Horizon Press, 1958.

Wright, Robert. *Non-Zero: The Logic of Human Destiny*. New York: Pantheon Books, 2000.

Wright, Robert. *A Short History of Progress*. New York: Carroll & Graf Publishers, 2004.

INDEX

TWO WORLDS VALUES

Beyond the evidential world of fear and "facts," lies the aspirational world of creativity and joy.

To feel the earth under out feet
To enjoy a primitive sense of shelter
To be embraced by intimate spaces
To see the horizon
To be relevant and visionary
To be surrounded by beauty
To be both alone and with others
To love and be loved
To practice and achieve
To work as a team
To be effective
To feel healthy and secure
To contribute to others
To live with passion
To be thankful
To experience life-long learning
To feel that we have given our all
To rest and regenerate
To celebrate design
To have faith in children
To believe in the future

TWO WORLDS COMMUNITY FOUNDATION

From the World of Design to the Deisgn of the World

We must extend design and stewardship to encompass all terrain. The new global city is now defined with zones of urban, suburban, rural, leisure and even "natural" precincts—all managed, all part of a designed system. Architects have tended to build pieces of cities without regarding their relationship to the whole. But holistic thinking is exactly what we need if we're ever to develop the capactiy to provide shelter on a global scale. It's clear that synthesis is not merely useful; it's critical.

—Bruce Mau
Massive Change